# Nevada Bucket List Adventure Guide

*Explore 100 Offbeat Destinations You Must Visit!*

**Alex Woods**

**Bridge Press**
support@bridgepress.org

**Please consider writing a review!**
Just visit: purplelink.org/review



ISBN: 978-1-955149-40-2

# FREE BONUS

Find Out 31 Incredible Places You Can Visit Next! Just Go to:

**purplelink.org/travel**

# Table of Contents

# How to Use This Book

Welcome to your very own adventure guide to exploring the many wonders of the state of Nevada. Not only does this book layout the most wonderful places to visit and sights to see in the vast state, but it also provides driving directions and GPS coordinates for Google Maps to make exploring that much easier.

**Adventure Guide**
Sorted by region, this guide offers over 100 amazing wonders found in Nevada for you to see and explore. These can be visited in any order, and this book will help keep track of where you've been and where to look forward to going next. Each portion describes the area or place, what to look for, how to get there, and what you may need to bring along.

**GPS Coordinates**
As you can imagine, not all of the locations in this book have a physical address. Fortunately, some of our listed wonders are either located within a national park or reserve, or are near a city, town, or place of business. For those that are not associated with a specific location, it is easiest to map it using GPS coordinates.

Luckily, Google has a system of codes that converts the coordinates into pin-drop locations that Google Maps is able to interpret and navigate.

Each adventure in this guide will include both the GPS coordinates and general directions on how to find the location.

It is important that you are prepared for poor cell signals. It's a good practice to route your location and ensure that the directions are accessible offline. Depending on your device and the distance of some locations, you may need to travel with a backup battery source.

# About Nevada

Known as the Silver State, Nevada was the 36th state to join the Union. It is called the Silver State because silver is a significant part of Nevada's history, where many prospectors went in search of fortune. It wasn't just silver that drew prospectors to mining; the famous Gold Rush also brought thousands to Nevada. The state is filled with ghost towns that used to support the mines and vibrant cities that adapted to other industries.

Nevada has gone through several changes over the years. The land started as the home of Native American tribes but was later settled by Americans moving from the east to the west. During exploration, three prominent Native American tribes inhabited the region: the Washoe, Paiute, and the Shoshone. Settlers also set up ranches and communities that promised Nevada was a land worth embracing.

Before long, the railroads found their way west, and Nevada was one of the places where improved infrastructure ensured better jobs and overall growth for the state. The Pony Express visited Nevada along the way, and stagecoach stops existed for settlers moving further west to California.

Today, Nevada is home to gaming, sports, outdoor activities, and some of America's most beautiful state and national parks. It is a perfect location for skiers, campers, and hikers from all over the world.

The name Nevada comes from the Spanish word meaning "snow covered." The Spanish, who were the first Europeans to explore the region, saw the snow-capped mountains and were reminded of the Sierra Nevada range in Spain. Therefore, they named the area Nevada.

The state bird is the sage hen, and the state flower is sagebrush. The flag bears the words "Battle Born" because Nevada became a state in 1864 during the American Civil War. The capital of Nevada is Carson City.

Many of the parks, trails, and outdoor attractions follow the "Leave no Trace" policies. Please be respectful and clean up after yourselves and your pets before leaving an area.

## Landscape and Climate

Nevada has a landscape that is mostly mountains and desert. The Sierra Nevada mountain range borders the state to the west, along with California. To the north, you will find Idaho and Oregon. Utah is to the east, and Arizona is southeast.

The climate of Nevada is mostly arid and dry, as a large part of the state is desert. Nevada gets the least amount of rainfall of any state. The mountains get more rain in the eastern and northeastern parts of the range.

With so much in the way of diversity, both in landscape and in culture, Nevada has become an epicenter of American life. There is much to explore and learn about the Silver State.

# Delamar Mountains Wilderness

Designated a wilderness area in 2004, the Delamar Mountains Wilderness is an excellent area for outdoor activities, including hiking, rock climbing, and rock scrambling. Camping is allowed for the adventurous traveler.

The area also contains a lot of twisting canyons and regions to explore. Dogs are welcome to explore this wilderness alongside their owners.

**Best Time to Visit:** Delamar Mountains Wilderness is accessible all year round.

**Pass/Permit/Fees:** It is free to enjoy Delamar Mountains Wilderness.

**Closest City or Town:** Alamo

**How to Get There:** From Alamo, take Broadway Street for 0.3 miles and turn right onto US-93 S. Continue on Alamo Canyon Road for 30.6 miles.

**GPS Coordinates:** 37.1840° N, -114.8559° W

**Did You Know?** Aside from seeing bighorn sheep and raptors, Delamar Mountains Wilderness is home to the endangered desert tortoise. Part of the wilderness is considered a Mormon Mesa Desert Tortoise Area of Critical Environmental Concern.

# South Pahroc Range Wilderness

South Pahroc Range Wilderness is 25,671 acres primarily used for hiking, backpacking, camping, and rock climbing. The multicolored volcanic rock found throughout this park was formed millions of years ago during several volcanic explosions. The South Pahroc Wilderness is an extremely rugged area within Nevada. There are deep canyons coupled with high ridges overlooking the area. There are golden eagles, mule deer, mountain lions, and prairie falcons roaming this wilderness.

**Best Time to Visit:** South Pahroc Range Wilderness is accessible all year round.

**Pass/Permit/Fees:** It is free to enter South Pahroc Range Wilderness.

**Closest City or Town:** Alamo

**How to Get There:** From Alamo, take Broadway Street and turn left onto US-93 N. Follow US-93 N until you reach South Pahroc Range Wilderness. For this location, we suggest bringing a map, as the remote access can be confusing.

**GPS Coordinates:** 37.4833° N, -115.0619° W

**Did You Know?** The range is made up of singular volcanic massifs and a compact group of mountains formed from volcanic explosions.

# Great Basin National Park

Located in the eastern part of Nevada, Great Basin National Park lies near the Utah border between the Wasatch Mountains and the Sierra Nevada in a region known as the Great Basin. The park is home to Wheeler Peak, a 13,065-foot summit and trail that overlooks all of Great Basin. It is the second tallest peak in the state of Nevada. Great Basin contains hiking trails, campgrounds, and the famous Lehman Caves, which are covered later in this guide. Dogs are allowed in the park, but only in the campgrounds.

**Best Time to Visit:** Great Basin is accessible all year round, but it's best in the winter months when the weather isn't too hot.

**Pass/Permit/Fees:** It is free to enter Great Basin National Park, but you need to pay to see the caves and take tours.

**Closest City or Town:** Baker

**How to Get There:** From Baker, head west on NV-488 toward Saval Avenue for 4.8 miles.

**GPS Coordinates:** 38.9300° N, -114.2634° W

**Did You Know?** The Bristlecone Trail brings you to a bristlecone pine that's known as Prometheus. It has grown for thousands of years. While on that same trail, continue a little further along, and you will see the only remaining glacier in Nevada: the Wheeler Peak Glacier.

# Lehman Caves

Located in the Great Basin National Park, President Warren G. Harding made the Lehman caves a natural landmark in the 1920s. The naturally formed caves contain lots of information about the ecology and geology of Nevada, which visitors can learn about on park ranger-guided tours for a small fee. Although filled with various rock formations and colors, the caves are primarily composed of white and gray limestone. As you travel through the galleries, you will see plenty of stalagmites and stalactites. Prospector Absalom Lehman discovered these caverns, and Clarence and Beatrice Rhodes were their first caretakers. They started giving people guided tours through the natural wonder before the caves became part of the Great Basin National Park in 1986. Unfortunately, dogs are not allowed at this attraction.

**Best Time to Visit:** Lehman Caves are accessible all year round.

**Pass/Permit/Fees:** Guided tours into the caves range from $12–$15. Reservations are required in advance.

**Closest City or Town:** Baker

**How to Get There:** From Baker, head west on NV-488 W toward Saval Avenue. In 5.5 miles, turn right into the Lehman Caves Visitors Center parking lot.

**GPS Coordinates:** 39.0054° N, -114.2207° W

**Did You Know?** It is believed that the caves served as a burial ground for the first Native Americans.

# Rhyolite Ghost Town

Founded in 1904 by Shorty Harris and E.L. Cross, Rhyolite was a booming gold-mining town that brought in $10,000 of gold ore per day. The town had a bank, a jail, and a red-light district that attracted women from as far as San Francisco. Rhyolite had one of the most successful mines—the Montgomery Shoshone mine. The town had dances, socials, a school for up to 250 children, an opera house, and an ice plant. There were two electric plants in the town. The town was called Rhyolite due to the rich volcanic soil. In 1907, there was a financial crisis, and the entire town was abandoned. There are still parts of the bank and jail standing, as well as a few other structures.

**Best Time to Visit:** It's best to visit Rhyolite between October and April.

**Pass/Permit/Fees:** It is free to access this ghost town.

**Closest City or Town:** Beatty

**How to Get There:** From Beatty, head southwest on Main Street onto State Highway 374 S. Turn right onto Rhyolite Road, and you will come right into the center of town.

**GPS Coordinates:** 36.9032° N, -116.8281° W

**Did You Know?** Rhyolite has been used as a movie set for Westerns. There is also a house made entirely of glass liquor and beer bottles that has been restored by a Hollywood studio.

# Gold Strike Hot Springs Trail Head

Gold Strike Hot Springs Trail is 6 miles out and back with heavy foot traffic. It is a challenging trail to hike because of the rocky terrain and steep cliffs. Consider taking a hiking buddy, wear sturdy shoes, and pack plenty of water for your hike. If you are an avid hiker, having the right gear for climbing is a must. There are waterfalls to see along the hike. Dogs are not allowed on the trail. The trail ultimately leads to the Colorado River, where the Hoover Dam forms what we know today as Lake Mead.

**Best Time to Visit:** The trail is best from October through May, as it gets far too hot in the summer. Always check the website for seasonal and weather closures.

**Pass/Permit/Fees:** It costs $25 to enter Lake Mead National Recreation Area.

**Closest City or Town:** Boulder City

**How to Get There:** From Boulder, head east on Arizona Street toward California Avenue. Turn left onto Avenue I, then turn right to stay on Avenue I. Turn right onto Nevada Way. In 0.7 miles, turn right onto US-93 BUS. Follow for 3.9 miles, then, at the traffic circle, take the first exit onto Goldstrike Canyon Road. Continue for 0.4 miles to reach the trailhead.

**GPS Coordinates:** 36.0098° N, -114.7689° W

**Did You Know?** Gold Strike Hot Springs Trail offers access to natural hot springs.

# Nature Discovery Trail and Rock Garden

Nature Discovery Trail and Rock Garden is located in Boulder City in the southeastern part of the state. The trail and garden are popular for younger kids, and the park offers a lot of educational information on desert animals in the area. This educational walk is only about 1,800 feet long and is lined with several rock statues representing local animals. These include a large jackrabbit, lizard, desert toad, frog, and scorpion. Each giant statue has a plaque at the bottom that gives scientific information about the animals.

**Best Time to Visit:** Nature Discovery Trail and Rock Garden are accessible all year round.

**Pass/Permit/Fees:** It is free to enter the trail and garden.

**Closest City or Town:** Boulder City

**How to Get There:** From Boulder City, head west on Arizona Street toward California Avenue. Turn right onto Nevada Way, then turn left onto Colorado Street. Make a left onto Boulder City Parkway. Turn right at the first cross street onto Industrial Road, then turn right onto Yucca Street. At the traffic circle, take the first exit to get to Nature Discovery Trail and Rock Garden.

**GPS Coordinates:** 35.9811° N, -114.8603° W

**Did You Know?** The trail ends at a picnic area where you can have a small lunch before moving on to your next adventure.

# River Mountain Loop Trail

River Mountain Loop Trail is a 34-mile paved loop trail. Located in Boulder City, the trail is great for wheelchairs, mobility equipment, and strollers. Certain parts of the trail are more challenging, as about 3.5 miles of this trail were once mining tracks on steep inclines. With great scenic views of Lake Mead and the surrounding area, it's a great place to bring the family to take in the natural wonders of Nevada. Dogs are allowed on this trail, but they must be kept on a leash. There is also very little shade here, so bring plenty of water, sunblock, and maybe a hat.

**Best Time to Visit:** River Mountain Loop Trail is accessible all year round.

**Pass/Permit/Fees:** If you access the trail through Lake Mead National Recreation Area, there will be a $25 entrance fee. Other parts of the trail are free to enter.

**Closest City or Town:** Boulder City

**How to Get There:** From Boulder City, take Nevada Way to State Highway 93. Turn right onto State Highway 93 and continue onto Lakeshore Road. The trailhead is located next to the Lake Mead Visitor Center. Prepare for tolls on this route.

**GPS Coordinates:** 36.0100° N, -114.7968° W

**Did You Know?** The asphalt trail was developed by the state and private developers so that visitors could see the wide splendor of the Lake Mead area.

# Tunnel Spring Wilderness

One of the smaller wilderness areas in Nevada, Tunnel Spring Wilderness, is just 5,000 acres of natural land. Visitors use the land for hiking and camping. The terrain can get rocky in certain spots, but overall, it is an easy hike and drive into the wilderness. There are mule deer, bighorn sheep, and mountain lions in the area. You will also see alpine trees throughout your hike. Tunnel Spring offers camping, hiking, climbing, and you may even see some horseback riders while you are in the park.

**Best Time to Visit:** Tunnel Spring Wilderness is accessible all year round.

**Pass/Permit/Fees:** It is free to visit this area.

**Closest City or Town:** Caliente

**How to Get There:** From Caliente, follow Lincoln Street and take a left onto US-93 N. Continue to follow US-93 N for 5.5 miles, then take a right onto Beaver Dam Road. Follow Beaver Dam Road for 26.6 miles until you reach Tunnel Spring Wilderness. This is a remote location, so pack a map and check against GPS coordinates before leaving.

**GPS Coordinates:**
37.5363° N, -114.0742° W

**Did You Know?** The highest elevations of Tunnel Spring are between 5,000 and 7,000 feet.

## Brewery Arts Center

Established in 1975, the Brewery Arts Center is a place where artists gather and work. The building was once the old Carson Brewing Company. Over time, the arts center purchased surrounding buildings, including a church, and built a center for all art forms. There is a black box theater, a proscenium theater, a painting arts center, and a large sculpture garden. A few years back, the street between the buildings was closed off, and there is now a two-block strip of outdoor space where artists and their collaborators can work and create. The center teaches art classes and has a music venue for concerts. It is privately funded and home to 17 different arts organizations.

**Best Time to Visit:** The Brewery Arts Center is available all year round.

**Pass/Permit/Fees:** It is free to enter, but you must pay for classes and shows.

**Closest City or Town:** Carson City

**How to Get There:** In Carson City, take W. 2nd Street to Thompson Street, turn right onto S. Division Street. Take a left onto W. King Street. The Brewery is on the left at 449 W. King Street.

**GPS Coordinates:** 39.1638° N, -119.7697° W

**Did You Know?** The art center received its name from the original building, the Carson Brewing Company, which opened in 1860 during the mining rush.

# Hang Gliding Tahoe

For thrill seekers, Hang Gliding Tahoe offers motorized hang gliders that sit one passenger and one instructor. The small aircrafts are FAA approved and safe for travel. From high above, you'll witness stunning views of the Sierra Nevada Range and Lake Tahoe. Flights take off from the Carson City airport, where your instructor will meet and join you on your flight. Not only are there gorgeous views during the warm weather months, but in the winter, you will see the snow-covered lake and surrounding area in all its splendor.

**Best Time to Visit:** Hang Gliding Tahoe is best in the summer, but it is available all year round.

**Pass/Permit/Fees:** Depending on which package you choose, Hang Gliding Tahoe prices range from $250–$450.

**Closest City or Town:** Carson City

**How to Get There:** From Carson City, head north on N. Carson Street toward W. Musser Street. Turn right onto E. William Street. Continue straight until the road changes to US-50 E. Turn left onto Airport Road, then left again onto E. College Parkway. You'll find Hang Gliding Tahoe at 2640 E. College Parkway.

**GPS Coordinates:** 39.1931° N, -119.7343° W

**Did You Know?** Even though you can't travel in the same aircraft, couples and families can all fly side by side during the tour.

# Jack C. Davis Observatory

The Jack C. Davis Observatory is an astrological observatory located on the Western Nevada College campus. The observatory has two reflecting telescopes and a third telescope with a spectrograph. There is also a dome on the observatory that has a refractor for studying sunspots. A weather station outside of the observatory collects data and sends it to Reno for analysis. The data is also published online for weather reports. The observatory hosts parties during specific astrological events, such as meteor showers and eclipses, that are open to the public.

**Best Time to Visit:** The observatory is open to the public on Saturday evenings until 11:00 p.m.

**Pass/Permit/Fees:** It is free to visit the Jack C. Davis Observatory.

**Closest City or Town:** Carson City

**How to Get There:** In Carson City, take N. Carson Street toward W. Musser Street. Turn left onto W. Winnie Lane, then right onto N. Ormsby Boulevard. Turn left to stay on N. Ormsby Boulevard. Turn left again onto Combs Canyon Road and then take another left onto Murphy Drive. Murphy Drive will become Vanpatten Avenue. Take a left after 0.2 miles and a right in 95 feet. The observatory will be on the left at 2269 Vanpatten Avenue.

**GPS Coordinates:** 39.1857° N, -119.7964° W

**Did You Know?** All of the telescopes are equipped with cameras that stream feeds for remote viewing.

# Kit Carson Trail

The Kit Carson Trail is a walking tour through the Nevada state capital of Carson City. The trail is a 2.5-mile-long self-guided tour that will take you past almost 60 different historic buildings, including the state capitol building. The Brewery Arts Center, the Bliss Mansion, and the Governor's Mansion are part of the tour as well. You will also see historic Victorian homes that belonged to some of the more prominent individuals and families that helped build Carson City.

**Best Time to Visit:** The trail is open all year round.

**Pass/Permit/Fees:** It costs $2.50 to buy a map for the trail. The trail turns into a ghost walk during October, costing $20 for adults and $10 for children ages 6–12.

**Closest City or Town:** Carson City

**How to Get There:** Once you get into Carson City, go to the Carson City Visitor Center on S. Carson Street to get a map of the tour route.

**GPS Coordinates:** 39.1495° N, -119.7698° W

**Did You Know?** Kit Carson played a crucial role in westward expansion, and he helped bring the United States to its current size. He married a Native American woman, and they had two children. Abraham Curry named the city after the Carson River and Kit Carson.

# Nevada State Railroad Museum

The Nevada State Railroad Museum is dedicated to the history and technology of the railroad system of Nevada. The museum is filled with artifacts, equipment, photos, and actual locomotives used during the building of the railroad. A lot of the exhibits are permanent, while others change throughout the year. There is also an opportunity to learn about steam and gas technology used to power locomotives.

Visitors can visit the actual trains that were first used on the railroad and learn about their history, how they were built, and who made them.

**Best Time to Visit:** The Nevada State Railroad Museum is available all year round, Thursday through Monday.

**Pass/Permit/Fees:** It costs $8 for adults to enter the museum. Children under 18 are free.

**Closest City or Town:** Carson City

**How to Get There:** Head south on S. Carson Street toward W. Musser Street. At the traffic circle, take the first exit and stay on S. Carson Street. In 0.3 miles, turn right onto Access Road, and the museum will be on the right at 2180 S. Carson Street.

**GPS Coordinates:** 39.0860° N, -119.4611° W

**Did You Know?** The locomotives at the museum still run on the rails. Tickets cost $8 for adults and are free for children.

# Shoe Tree Brewing Company

The Shoe Tree Brewing Company is located in Carson City. It was founded in 2017, brothers Jeff and Paul Young started the business. The brewery has 18 different beers on tap as well as 16 growlers and 14 different canned beers. All the beers are brewed right there at Shoe Tree. The brewery has also been the recipient of over 22 medals in the art of beer brewing.

**Best Time to Visit:** Shoe Tree Distillery is available and open all year round.

**Pass/Permit/Fees:** There is no cover charge to enter the brewery.

**Closest City or Town:** Carson City

**How to Get There:** From downtown Carson City, take N. Carson Street toward W. Musser Street. Turn right onto Hot Springs Road, then left onto N. Roop Street. Turn right onto E. College Parkway. Next, take a left onto Research Way. Turn left onto Old Hot Springs Road. The destination will be on the right.

**GPS Coordinates:** 39.1939° N, -119.7526° W

**Did You Know?** Shoe Tree Brewing Company sits on the same land as the Carson Hot Springs. The hot springs are a natural geothermal pool that pumps 60 gallons of hot water per minute. The average temperature of the water is 120°F. There is also a resort where you can rent rooms and spend days soaking in the natural springs.

# The Children's Museum of Northern Nevada

The Children's Museum of Northern Nevada is a place where young children can learn through interaction and play. The museum has a play-based philosophy where children from infants to young teens are encouraged to use their imagination as families come together to learn about the humanities, arts, and sciences. On the first floor of the museum, there is a spaceship and sheriff's office. Kids can dress up in costumes, play with toys, and explore a trivia board of exciting facts. In the basement, there is a display of sharks for kids to learn about the ocean's predators. There is also an art room for kids to draw and paint. For the child who loves science, there is a STEM room and STEM camp available.

**Best Time to Visit:** The Children's Museum of Nevada is open all year long. It is closed on Sunday.

**Pass/Permit/Fees:** The museum accepts donations.

**Closest City or Town:** Carson City

**How to Get There:** The museum is located in the heart of downtown Carson City across the street from the Nevada State Museum Carson City location.

**GPS Coordinates:** 39.1688° N, -119.7664° W

**Did You Know?** The building that houses the Children's Museum of Northern Nevada used to be the home of the Carson City Civic Auditorium.

## The Foreman-Roberts House Museum

The Foreman-Roberts House is a historic landmark and museum in Carson City. Initially built in Washoe City, the house was moved to Carson City during the Gold Rush on the flatbed of a locomotive. The house is one of the last surviving Gothic Revival homes in Nevada. It is known for its gingerbread bargeboard and steep-sloped roof. Before settling in Nevada, James D. Roberts moved west during the Gold Rush and lived in several places while mining for gold. The last of his descendants to live in the house left the home to the city in 1969. The city was going to demolish the house to make way for a park, but citizens rallied to save the home and make it into a museum.

**Best Time to Visit:** The Foreman-Roberts House Museum is open all year long on the weekends.

**Pass/Permit/Fees:** It is free to visit the Foreman-Roberts House Museum.

**Closest City or Town:** Carson City

**How to Get There:** The house is in the heart of downtown Carson City on N. Carson Street. Take Interstate 580 N to State Highway 395 S to reach it.

**GPS Coordinates:** 39.1719° N, -119.7667° W

**Did You Know?** The last woman to live in the house was Hattie Roberts, a direct descendant of patriot Nathan Hale. When the city took over the home in 1969, Hale's direct orders from George Washington to join the Revolutionary War still hung on the wall.

## Washoe Lake State Park

Washoe Lake State Park is located in Washoe County. The park offers hiking, camping, walking, equestrian sports, water sports, and a bunch of other outdoor activities. It is located in a scenic valley with breathtaking views of the Sierra Nevada, Carson, and Virginia mountain ranges. There are 49 camping sites in Washoe Lake State Park that are very popular. Surrounding areas do not offer camping, so after people are done hiking and exploring other parts of the state park's location, they come to Washoe Lake to camp for the night.

**Best Time to Visit:** Washoe Lake State Park is open and accessible all year round.

**Pass/Permit/Fees:** It costs $5 for Nevada vehicles to enter Washoe Lake State Park. It costs $10 for non-Nevada residents.

**Closest City or Town:** Carson City

**How to Get There:** From Carson City, head north on N. Carson Street toward W. Musser Street. Merge onto I-580. Take Exit 10 toward Eastlake Boulevard, then turn right onto Eastlake Boulevard. Washoe Lake State Park is on the left at 4855 Eastlake Boulevard.

**GPS Coordinates:** 39.2420° N, -119.7639° W

**Did You Know?** The American Discovery Trail covers 500 miles of Nevada's rustic backcountry.

# Dayton State Park

Dayton State Park is located at the foot of the Virginia Range. Next to the Carson River, the park offers a lot of natural beauty and outdoor activities. The park used to be a fishing camp for the first Native Americans living in the area—the Paiute Tribe.

The hiking at Dayton State Park is breathtaking and offers a lot in the way of wildlife. You will see hawks, foxes, and maybe even some porcupines on your hike. It is also a great place to camp and includes an area for RVs with grills for barbecuing. Picnicking is allowed throughout the park.

**Best Time to Visit:** Dayton State Park is open all year round.

**Pass/Permit/Fees:** It costs $5 to enter Dayton State Park if you have a Nevada vehicle. Non-Nevada vehicles cost $10 to enter.

**Closest City or Town:** Dayton

**How to Get There:** From Dayton, head south on Shady Lane toward Tyler. Turn left onto Main Street, then take another left onto US-50 E. The park will be less than a mile down US-50 on the right.

**GPS Coordinates:** 39.2491° N, -119.5876° W

**Did You Know?** Dayton State Park is the home of an old mill that was used during the days of the rush for precious metals. Parts of the structure still stand.

# Fort Churchill

Fort Churchill is a historic state park in the northern part of Nevada. The fort was built to protect the Pony Express riders as they were delivering mail out west. The park was also a waystation and a place for prospectors to rest during their travels.

The park offers camping, hiking, and beautiful views of northern Nevada on 3,200 acres situated along the Carson River. Other outdoor activities include horseback riding, bird watching, and canoeing.

**Best Time to Visit:** Fort Churchill is open and available all year round.

**Pass/Permit/Fees:** For Nevada vehicles, the fee to enter Fort Churchill is $5. For non-Nevada vehicles, the fee to enter Fort Churchill is $10.

**Closest City or Town:** Dayton

**How to Get There:** From Dayton, take Main Street to US-50 E. Follow US-50 E for 20.3 miles, then take a right onto Ramsey Cutoff. In 3.4 miles, turn right onto US-95 ALT S, and then in another 4.2 miles, take a right onto Fort Churchill Road. Turn left at the fork. There are two parking lots off of this road on either side of the monument. A trail connects the monument to the park.

**GPS Coordinates:** 39.2944° N, -119.2677° W

**Did You Know?** You can explore the ruins and see life in the 1800s.

# Elko Hot Springs

Elko is the biggest city within Elko County. Elko is known as a hub of activity for those who seek outdoor adventure and activities. The city and county are home to the Ruby Mountains and Lamoille Canyon. The town was founded by the Central Pacific Railroad. Elko is a center for commerce and revenue in the Ruby Valley. It was founded because it was located at the end of the railroad. It was first inhabited in 1868 and was located along what was known as the California Trail. Elko is home to two hot springs: the Hot Hole and the Elko Hot Spring. Both of the springs are easily accessible by anyone who wants to walk in. The springs are located next to the Humboldt River.

**Best Time to Visit:** The Elko hot springs are accessible all year round.

**Pass/Permit/Fees:** There are no fees to the hot springs.

**Closest City or Town:** Elko

**How to Get There:** From Elko, head southeast on 5th St and turn right onto Silver St. Take a left onto Errecart Blvd, right onto Bullion Rd, and the hot springs will be on the left.

**GPS Coordinates:** 40.8324° N, -115.7631° W.

**Did You Know?** The hot springs have been around for centuries.

# Lamoille Canyon

One of the most beautiful natural wonders in all of Nevada, Lamoille Canyon was formed by the movement of glaciers over 250,000 years ago. The canyon offers a byway where you can drive and see some of the most spectacular natural views in the area. This expanse offers almost every outdoor activity imaginable.

**Best Time to Visit:** Lamoille Canyon is accessible all year round, but the best time to visit is between the spring and fall when the area has lots of flowers and color.

**Pass/Permit/Fees:** A $6 permit is required to explore Lamoille Canyon. There is also a $3 recreation fee per person.

**Closest City or Town:** Elko

**How to Get There:** From Elko, head southeast on NV-227 E. At the traffic circle, continue straight onto NV-227. Turn right onto NF-660. Lamoille Canyon is on the right.

**GPS Coordinates:** 40.6916° N, -115.4742° W

**Did You Know?** While in the canyon, you can hike, bike, backpack, rock climb, snow ski, snowmobile, or take a scenic drive through the byway. There are several kinds of wildflowers and alpine trees, along with animals like deer and grouse.

# Ruby Mountains

The Ruby Mountains, nicknamed "Nevada's Yosemite," are located in Elko County. The mountains are the ideal outdoor location. With vast views, miles of trails, a plethora of trees and wildlife, and sweeping canyons, the Ruby Mountains have something to offer everyone. Dogs are allowed on some of the trails, but always check beforehand to make sure. Locals refer to the mountains as "the Rubies." There is so much outdoor activity here. The activities are split between the winter and summer. In the winter, you can snowmobile, cross-country ski, and hike. In the warmer weather months, you can camp, climb, fish, horseback ride, hunt, bike, ride four-wheelers, and take scenic drives.

**Best Time to Visit:** The Ruby Mountains are accessible year-round, but the best time to visit is during the spring through the fall when the leaves change color.

**Pass/Permit/Fees:** It is free to enter the Ruby Mountains wilderness.

**Closest City or Town:** Elko

**How to Get There:** Take Highway 227 to the Lamoille Canyon Scenic Byway to access the Ruby Mountains.

**GPS Coordinates:** 40.6219° N, -115.4750° W

**Did You Know?** Avid visitors recommend the Soldier Basin Trail, which accesses lakes, trout fishing, and beautiful scenery.

# Becky Peak Wilderness

Becky Peak Wilderness spans 18,119 acres and is best for camping, hiking, backpacking, hunting, and horseback riding. Dogs are allowed to accompany you on your trip.

There are many wildflowers and plants in the wilderness, including sagebrush, larkspur, and prickly pear cactus. On the higher elevations, you will find bristlecone and pine trees. Animals you may spot on your hikes are mule deer, lizards, and some wild horses.

**Best Time to Visit:** Becky Peak Wilderness is accessible all year round.

**Pass/Permit/Fees:** It is free to enter the Becky Peak Wilderness.

**Closest City or Town:** Ely

**How to Get There:** Becky Peak Wilderness is located off of Highway 93 N.

**GPS Coordinates:** 39.9588° N, -114.6130° W

**Did You Know?** You can hike up to the top of Becky Peak, which stands at 9,859 feet. The lowest elevation is 6,500 feet.

# Goshute Canyon Wilderness

Goshute Canyon Wilderness is 42,544 acres of open land. Abundant in wildflowers, the area also boasts limestone cliffs great for climbing, bouldering, and caving.

Located in the Cherry Creek Range, the wilderness contains the Goshute Canyon, which is home to several species of trout. Camping and dogs are welcome.

**Best Time to Visit:** Accessible all year round, Goshute Canyon is best from the spring through the fall when the flowers are in bloom.

**Pass/Permit/Fees:** It is free to enter Goshute Canyon Wilderness.

**Closest City or Town:** Ely

**How to Get There:** From Ely, follow US-93 N to State Hwy 489. Continue on State Highway 489 for 20.9 miles until you reach Goshute Canyon Wilderness.

**GPS Coordinates:** 40.0520° N, -114.8513° W

**Did You Know?** The hidden Goshute Canyon has several trout-filled streams that flow through the area. There is a network of limestone caves throughout the canyon. The caving is not too difficult, and it's a perfect trek for first-time spelunkers. What's most important about Goshute Canyon Wilderness is the variety of colors you will see, from yellow flowers to dark, stone-colored ridges.

# Bristlecone Wilderness

Designated a wilderness area in 2006, Bristlecone Wilderness covers 14,095 acres of land and is ideal for hiking, climbing, and camping. While on top of the mountain, you can see sweeping views of the Schell Creek Range, Steptoe Valley, and lots of pinyon pines and juniper. The lower lands have a variety of grasses and desert brush. While hiking and backpacking through the area, you may see pronghorn antelope and mule deer. There have also been some bighorn sheep spotted in the area. The Bristlecone Wilderness contains Heusser Mountain and a variety of plants and animals. Camping is permitted, and dogs are welcome to accompany you.

**Best Time to Visit:** Bristlecone Wilderness is accessible all year round, but it's best in the springtime when the wildflowers are in full bloom.

**Pass/Permit/Fees:** It is free to enter the wilderness.

**Closest City or Town:** Ely

**How to Get There:** From Ely, head east on E. Aultman Street toward 7th Street E until you hit US-93 N. In 7.7 miles, turn left onto White Pine County Road. Stay on White Pine County Road until you reach Bristlecone Wilderness on the right.

**GPS Coordinates:** 39.3959° N, -114.8830° W

**Did You Know?** Heusser Mountain stands at 9,409 feet.

# High Schells Wilderness

High Schells Wilderness area is 121,497 acres of land in the Humboldt-Toiyabe National Forest. It was designated a wilderness area in 2006, and it has some of the most beautiful views in Nevada. North Schell Peak tops out at 11,880 feet. The peak rises high above the timberline. At that height, you will have great views of the surrounding area, including South Schell Peak and Taft Peak. There are also clear streams that run through the valleys of the area, and you can also see the South Snake Range, which is a mountain range surrounded by desert. Dogs can accompany you in the wilderness area, but some of the hikes take you to high elevations, so if your dog can't hike that high, it is best to leave them behind. There are campgrounds in the wilderness. The area is best for hiking and backpacking.

**Best Time to Visit:** High Schells Wilderness is accessible all year round. There are snowy peaks in this area all the time, so dress accordingly if exploring high elevations.

**Pass/Permit/Fees:** It is free to enter the wilderness.

**Closest City or Town:** Ely

**How to Get There:** From Ely, turn left onto Highway 893, which can be accessed from Highway 93. Take a left onto NF-433. Follow NF-433 to High Schells Wilderness.

**GPS Coordinates:** 39.3647° N, -114.6010° W

**Did You Know?** Ely was founded during the days of the Pony Express.

# Quinn Canyon Wilderness

Quinn Canyon Wilderness includes 26,256 acres of protected land as part of the Humboldt-Toiyabe National Forest. The canyon is a transition point between the desert and low and high elevations. The top of the range has many colored rocks that are a result of the chemical makeup of the stone. Several small waterfalls sprout from the canyon, and while in the mountain range, you may see bighorn sheep, mountain lions, and coyotes. There is also a plethora of bristlecone pines.

**Best Time to Visit:** Quinn Canyon is accessible all year round.

**Pass/Permit/Fees:** It is free to enter the state park.

**Closest City or Town:** Ely

**How to Get There:** From Ely, head south on Great Basin Boulevard toward Avenue G. Turn right onto US-6 W. Follow for 62.3 miles, then turn left onto R R Valley Road. In 5 miles, turn right. In 2.3 miles, take another right. Stay onto NF-410 until it turns to NF-410. Take a slight right onto NF-411, then follow for 3.7 miles to Quinn Canyon Wilderness. There are unmarked roads, so it is advised to pack a map.

**GPS Coordinates:** 38.1202° N, -115.7095° W

**Did You Know?** The wilderness contains many drainages that carry melted ice and rain down the sides of the mountain range.

# Schellback Wilderness

Schellback Wilderness is 36,151 acres of land located in the Northeast White Pine Range. Part of the Humboldt-Toiyabe National Forest, the wilderness is home to many native animals and plants of Nevada. While making your way through the area, you will have full access to seeing all of the flora and fauna. Established in 2006, the site is located north of Bald Mountain.

The wilderness is best suited for hiking, climbing, camping, and backpacking. Dogs are welcome to join you on your trip. The eastern slope of the wilderness area is desert-like; however, if you go onto the western side of Schellback, you will find lush vegetation and several natural springs.

**Best Time to Visit:** Schellback is accessible all year round.

**Pass/Permit/Fees:** It is free to enter Shellback Wilderness.

**Closest City or Town:** Ely

**How to Get There:** From Ely, head west on US-50 W. Turn left onto NF-401, then take another left at the first cross street. Continue onto NF-400 until you reach Schellback Wilderness.

**GPS Coordinates:** 39.346815° N, -115.3551368° W

**Did You Know?** The Northeast White Pine Ridge stands at over 9,000 feet tall, giving hikers a great view of the region. There are limestone rock formations that are the home to pinion juniper.

# Sand Mountain

Sand Mountain is a large dune in the western part of Nevada. It is the largest continuous sand dune in the Great Basin, and it measures 600 feet tall and 3.5 miles long. The area is mostly used for ATVs and off-roading. There are designated trails for different activities, which were created to save the Sand Mountain blue butterfly habitat.

The sands forming the dunes were once the bottom of Lake Lahontan, which dried up around 9,000 years ago. The prehistoric lake dominated most of the Nevada terrain. Camping is allowed in the area, but there is no water, so bring plenty regardless of whether you plan to stay overnight or just pass through.

**Best Time to Visit:** Sand Mountain is accessible all year round.

**Pass/Permit/Fees:** It costs $40 to enter Sand Mountain.

**Closest City or Town:** Fallon

**How to Get There:** From Fallon, head east on US-50 E toward N. Nevada Street, then continue for 26 miles. Take a left and follow for 1.8 more miles to reach Sand Mountain.

**GPS Coordinates:** 39.3085° N, -118.3971° W

**Did You Know?** In 1860, the Pony Express built a station in Sand Mountain.

## Scripps State Wildlife Management Area

Scripps State Wildlife Management Area is located in the northwestern part of Nevada by Reno, Sparks, and Carson City. The highest elevation in the park is 5,023 feet, which is great for long hikes. This is an ideal place to take in Nevada's wilderness. There is a parking lot next to the area. If you have binoculars, bring them along for a chance to see birds, bighorn sheep, and mountain lions.

**Best Time to Visit:** Scripps State Wildlife Management Area is open year-round, but certain parts shut down between February and August.

**Pass/Permit/Fees:** It is free to enjoy Scripps Wildlife Management Area. If you enter through Washoe State Park, there is a $5 fee.

**Closest City or Town:** Reno

**How to Get There:** From Reno, take Interstate Highway 80 E to Exit 15 for Interstate Highway 580 S. Take Exit 25B onto Virginia Street S. Make a left onto Eastlake Boulevard, then turn right onto Lakeshore Drive. Turn right onto County Road 233, and make a right onto County Road. The entrance for Scripps State Wildlife Management Area is straight ahead.

**GPS Coordinates:** 39.2968° N, -119.8024° W

**Did You Know?** There is no camping allowed in Scripps State Wildlife Management Area. If you want to camp, you can do so next door at Washoe State Park.

# Fernley 95A Speedway

The Fernley 95A Speedway is located in Fernley, just outside of Reno. The dirt track caters to mostly off-road racing. The speedway hosts events by the National Sprint Car Racing Series, as well as go-kart racing. In the heart of a basin, the track grants sweeping views of the surrounding skies and desert. The Fernley Speedway is a much-loved attraction for locals.

**Best Time to Visit:** Fernley Speedway is best from March to October when the track sees the bulk of its events.

**Pass/Permit/Fees:** Event prices vary, so it is best to check the website before visiting.

**Closest City or Town:** Fernley

**How to Get There:** From Fernley, head east on W. Main Street toward East Street. Turn right onto US-50 ALT W. In 4.6 miles, take a right. Continue straight, and the speedway will be on the left at 1965 S. Highway 95A.

**GPS Coordinates:** 39.5407° N, -119.2357° W

**Did You Know?** Fernley 95A Speedway is also a campground. You can park your RV there or dry camp around the track and watch races from your site.

# Fernley Wildlife Management Area

The Fernley Wildlife Management Area is an expanse dedicated to hiking, camping, and wildlife. Located in northern Nevada, several moderate-to-difficult hiking trails wind through grasslands and creeks under open blue skies with mountains sloping in the distance. It's a good idea to bring plenty of water, sunblock, a hat, and sunglasses.

**Best Time to Visit:** Fernley Wildlife Management Area is accessible all year round.

**Pass/Permit/Fees:** It is free to enter Fernley Wildlife Management Area.

**Closest City or Town:** Fernley

**How to Get There:** From Fernley, head west on I-80 W, then take the ramp onto I-80 E. Take Exit 50 for Nevada Pacific Parkway. Turn left onto Duffy Road. Continue straight for 4.4 miles, and you will find the Fernley Wildlife Management Area.

**GPS Coordinates:** 39.6279° N, -119.1221° W

**Did You Know?** The park is at an elevation of 4,016 feet

# Out of Town Park

Located in Fernley, Out of Town Park covers about 50 acres of land and offers various family activities. You can play games, picnic, and spend time with loved ones. The park is centrally located by a major highway, making it easy to find and enjoy. There are horseshoe pits, a bandstand shell, and a small dance area for live shows and entertainment. For kids, there are concession stands, little league fields, tee-ball fields, soccer fields, and several playgrounds. A lot of families utilize the picnic areas for eating, gathering, and celebrating.

**Best Time to Visit:** Out of Town Park is accessible and open all year round.

**Pass/Permit/Fees:** It is free to enter and enjoy Out of Town Park.

**Closest City or Town:** Fernley

**How to Get There:** In Fernley, head east on W. Main Street toward East Street. Keep right to continue toward Farm District Road, then merge. In 0.2 miles, turn left to reach Out of Town Park.

**GPS Coordinates:** 39.6010° N, -119.2229° W

**Did You Know?** Out of Town Park is also the home of the Fernley rodeo grounds. While enjoying the park, you can also take in the rodeo and watch cowboys at their best.

# Berlin-Ichthyosaur State Park

Berlin-Ichthyosaur State Park offers history and outdoor activities. There are hiking trails and camping available in this vast park of trees and animals.

Berlin-Ichthyosaur State Park is home to the ghost town of Berlin. It was a mining town before the mine was abandoned. Dogs are allowed to visit the park, but they must be kept on a leash that cannot exceed 6 feet in length.

**Best Time to Visit:** Berlin-Ichthyosaur State Park is accessible all year round. Check the website for temporary closures.

**Pass/Permit/Fees:**
For Nevada residents, it is $5 to enter the park. It is $10 for non-Nevada residents.

**Closest City or Town:** Gabbs

**How to Get There:** From Gabbs, head east on Brucite Street toward Lindsay Lane for 0.2 miles. Turn left onto NV-361 N. Turn right onto NV-844 E. Take a slight right onto Berlin Road. Follow Berlin Road to Berlin-Ichthyosaur State Park.

**GPS Coordinates:** 38.8720° N, -117.5936° W

**Did You Know?** The park gets its name from the Ichthyosaur, a prehistoric reptile that swam in the warm waters of a lake that was once in Nevada about 225,000 years ago. There is a fossil house where you can see remains discovered in the area.

# Bonsai Rock

Bonsai Rock is a massive granite boulder that sits off of Lake Tahoe's shore. The boulder is a popular spot for jumping into the water and swimming. However, it doesn't get too busy because there is no real parking around the area, so many tourists choose to swim elsewhere. This is a nice, quiet spot to enjoy nature. There is no actual trail that goes to Bonsai Rock, so you have to find it on your GPS or map and hike your way there. Bonsai Rock received its name on account of small trees naturally sprouting through the cracks in the rock. It is believed that there is limited root growth due to the rock density.

**Best Time to Visit:** Bonsai Rock is best in the summer months from May to October when the weather is warm enough for swimming.

**Pass/Permit/Fees:** It costs $10 to enter Lake Tahoe National Park.

**Closest City or Town:** Genoa

**How to Get There:** From Genoa, head east on Nixon Street, and turn left onto Jacks Valley Road. Use the left two lanes to turn left onto US-395 N. Continue for 1.2 miles to S. Carson Street. In 0.2 miles, turn left onto US-50 W. Follow for 9.8 miles, then turn right onto NV-28 S. Follow for 6.7 miles to Bonsai Rock.

**GPS Coordinates:** 39.1847° N, -119.9281° W

**Did You Know?** The rock is best used for cliff jumping as there is no beach or hiking trail around the area.

# Lake Tahoe

Lake Tahoe, the most famous lake in all of Nevada, is located on the state line of Nevada and California. The lake was formed about 2 million years ago and has not changed in size in the past 1 million years. The landscape surrounding the water is believed to have developed 10,000 years ago. As a basin, the lake was created when there was a sink between two mountain ranges after several volcanic explosions. Lake Tahoe is the second-deepest lake in the United States. Its official depth is 1,645 feet, although there is much speculation regarding this number as many believe the bottom has yet to be discovered.

**Best Time to Visit:** Lake Tahoe has activities available year round.

**Pass/Permit/Fees:** It costs $10 per vehicle to enter Lake Tahoe State Park.

**Closest City or Town:** Genoa, Nevada

**How to Get There:** From Genoa, head east on Nixon Street toward Jacks Valley Road/Main Street. Turn right onto NV-206 S, then turn right onto NV-207 W. Take a sharp right onto US-50 E, and follow to Lake Tahoe. There are other routes to reach Lake Tahoe, as it is a large lake that touches many different cities.

**GPS Coordinates:** 39.0097° N, -119.9460° W

**Did You Know?** There is a myth that a Loch Ness–type monster lives in the lake. The monster was nicknamed "Tessie."

# Lam Watah Nature Trail

Located by the ancient and dazzling Lake Tahoe, Lam Watah Nature Trail is a 2.8-mile, relatively easy hike. The trail is partially paved with a wide variety of wildflowers lining the path. It is good to keep in mind that there is a lot of foot traffic. The trail ends at a Lake Tahoe beach, where there is access to various outdoor recreation. Dogs are allowed on this trail, but must be kept on a leash.

**Best Time to Visit:** Accessible all year round, Lam Watah Nature Trail is best from the months of May through October.

**Pass/Permit/Fees:** It costs $5 to enter the Lake Tahoe Basin.

**Closest City or Town:** Genoa

**How to Get There:** From Genoa, head east on Nixon Street toward Jacks Valley Road. Turn right onto NV-206 S. In 5.6 miles, turn right onto NV-207 W. Take a sharp right onto US-50 E in 11 miles. Turn left onto Kahle Drive, and the trail will be on the right at 193 Kahle Drive.

**GPS Coordinates:** 38.9709° N, -119.9359° W

**Did You Know?** Lake Tahoe has been around for millions of years and is one of the deepest lakes in North America.

# Sand Harbor

Sand Harbor is a beautiful natural spot on the eastern shore of Lake Tahoe. The harbor offers terrain of smooth rocks and a beach for enjoying the lake. It was once the home of the Washoe Native American tribe. They would spend their days fishing and hunting. Lake Tahoe is a stunning blue lake that sits high atop the Sierra Nevada mountain range. Sand Harbor is part of Lake Tahoe's extremely diverse topography, ranging from tall peaks to meadows and forests around the lake's perimeter.

**Best Time to Visit:** Sand Harbor is best in the summer months when you can fish, kayak, swim, cliff jump, and paddleboard, among other summer activities.

**Pass/Permit/Fees:** It costs $10 to enter Lake Tahoe State Park.

**Closest City or Town:** Genoa

**How to Get There:** From Genoa, head east on Nixon Street, and take a left onto Jacks Valley Road. Use the left two lanes to turn onto US-395 N. Continue onto S. Carson Street. Use the left two lanes to turn onto US-50 W. Follow for 9.8 miles, then turn right onto NV-28 S. Follow to Sand Harbor Beach.

**GPS Coordinates:** 39.1985° N, -119.9323° W

**Did You Know?** Sand Harbor was transformed after Europeans discovered the area in the 1840s. By the 1870s, it had become a logging area where wood and lumber were transported through an intricate system of flumes.

# Black Rock Desert

Located in the Black Rock Desert–High Rock Canyon Emigrant Trails National Conservation Area, Black Rock is 314,835 acres of protected desert playas. Its name came from the lava beds that were formed hundreds of thousands of years ago. Motorized vehicles are not allowed through the lava beds, so the area is best for hiking and backpacking. Camping is permitted, and many people say that the area offers some of the most isolated and expansive experiences they have ever had.

**Best Time to Visit:** Black Rock Desert is accessible all year round, but it is best in the cooler weather months when it's not too hot.

**Pass/Permit/Fees:** It is free to enter the Black Rock Desert.

**Closest City or Town:** Gerlach

**How to Get There:** From Gerlach, head southeast on Main Street toward Beechnut Court. Continue onto NV-447 S. Turn left onto Jungo Road, and follow for 22.7 miles. Turn left, then left again in 0.2 miles. In 1.6 miles, turn right. In 7.4 miles, turn left and follow for 5.7 miles to Black Rock Desert. There are unmarked roads, so it is advised to bring a map.

**GPS Coordinates:** 40.9107° N, -119.0560° W

**Did You Know?** Black Rock Desert is the home of the Burning Man festival. Plan your trip accordingly.

# Fly Geyser

Fly Geyser is a geothermal phenomenon. As its name suggests, it is a geyser of hot water that blasts up from the ground 5 feet into the air. It is unique because, unlike other geysers, it never stops shooting water. In addition to Fly Geyser, there are other geysers located in the area. Since these are on private property, you must make a reservation for a guided walking tour. These tours are 3 miles long on uneven ground, so make sure to wear sturdy shoes and have some protection from the sun.

**Best Time to Visit:** Fly Geyser is accessible all year round.

**Pass/Permit/Fees:** You must make a reservation to see the geysers. There are morning walks year round and evening walks during the summer months. It costs $40 to reserve a ticket for the tour. Children under 12 years of age are free.

**Closest City or Town:** Gerlach

**How to Get There:** From Gerlach, head northwest onto County Road 447 for 0.4 miles, then continue straight onto County Road 34 N for 19.5 miles. Turn right, and Fly Geyser will be on your left.

**GPS Coordinates:** 40.8594° N, -119.3319° W

**Did You Know?** A company that was drilling accidentally formed the geysers. Calcium carbonate built up, and it now surrounds the geyser in brilliant colors of red and green.

# Massacre Rim

Massacre Rim is a Dark Sky Sanctuary. It is best known for its camping because of the number of stars you can see at night. Although there are no developed trails in the park, patrons are encouraged to go off-trail hiking and discover the wonders of the area.

Massacre Rim is so remote that you can see some of the brightest stars. It is one of the darkest places on Earth. There is almost no light at night, and the stars get so bright that they cast a shadow.

**Best Time to Visit:** Massacre Rim is available all year round.

**Pass/Permit/Fees:** It is free to enter Massacre Rim.

**Closest City or Town:** Gerlach

**How to Get There:** Massacre Rim is located near County Highway 34. The rim is extremely remote, so verify your driving directions with a GPS and pack a map before leaving.

**GPS Coordinates:** 41.69133° N, -119.621529° W

**Did You Know?** Astronomers have discovered and studied new parts of the Milky Way galaxy by staying at Massacre Rim.

# Trego Hot Springs

Discovered in the 1860s, Trego Hot Springs is a collection of natural geothermal pools located in Black Rock. These pools started as natural springs, but over time, many of them were altered by hand to make them more usable.

The land is public, so anyone can drive up to the springs and take a long soak in the 187°F water. Leashed dogs are allowed around the easily accessible area, but they are not permitted in the springs.

**Best Time to Visit:** Trego Hot Springs are available all year round.

**Pass/Permit/Fees:** It is free to enjoy Trego Hot Springs.

**Closest City or Town:** Gerlach

**How to Get There:** From Gerlach, head southeast on Main Street toward Beechnut Court. In 0.4 miles, continue onto NV-447 S. Turn left onto Jungo Road and continue for 16.6 miles. Turn left. Take another slight left onto Trego Road. This is a remote destination, so it is advised to pack a map.

**GPS Coordinates:** 40.7716° N, -119.1167° W

**Did You Know?** At one time, the Western Pacific Railroad ran a station near the springs.

# Whitney Mesa Nature Preserve

Located in Clark County, the Whitney Mesa Nature Preserve has long been seen as a respite away from the hustle and flow of the cities. Whitney Mesa is mainly known for its wide-open spaces that allow visitors to roam for miles uninhibited. The preserve also includes the Whitney Mesa Nature Preserve Trail, a popular hiking trail among the local residents. Parts of the path are wheelchair accessible. Dogs are allowed in the preserve as long as they are kept on a leash. There are several additional activities available in the education center.

**Best Time to Visit:** Whitney Mesa Nature Preserve is accessible all year round. It is open from 6 a.m. to midnight.

**Pass/Permit/Fees:** It is free to enter Whitney Mesa Nature Preserve, but there are fees for some activities.

**Closest City or Town:** Henderson

**How to Get There:** From Henderson, continue onto I-515 N. Take the I-515 N exit from NV-564 W/E. Lake Mead Parkway. Take Exit 65 and continue onto E. Russell Road. Take Galleria Drive to Patrick Lane. You'll arrive at Whitney Mesa Nature Preserve in 1.2 miles.

**GPS Coordinates:** 36.0729° N, -115.0511° W

**Did You Know?** The preserve is home to desert animals like tortoises and bighorn sheep. You will also see plants like sagebrush along your hikes.

# Thunderbird Preservation Society

The Thunderbird Preservation Society was created after the death of George Whittell Jr. in 1969. George purchased a vast portion of land on the eastern shore of Lake Tahoe. He had plans to build a ski resort, a summer estate, and a one-million-dollar casino. George fell in love with nature and decided to keep his land as it was. When he died, a man named Jack Dreyfus purchased the estate and gave it to the state of Nevada. Today, George's Thunderbird Lodge is still standing, and you can visit it and take tours. A lot of the structures are used for events, weddings, dinners, and school class trips. In 2000, the land was deemed a historic landmark.

**Best Time to Visit:** Thunderbird estate is open all year.

**Pass/Permit/Fees:** Tickets must be purchased for any tours or events at Thunderbird Estate. Donations are always welcome.

**Closest City or Town:** Incline Village

**How to Get There:** From Incline Village, take Highway 28 S to George Whittell Road, which ends at Thunderbird Lodge.

**GPS Coordinates:** 39.1025° N, -119.5510° W

**Did You Know?** There is a high-speed wooden yacht at the lodge called the Thunderbird Yacht. Its main purpose is to bring people all around the lake as fast as possible. George Whittell had it built for his personal collection of planes and boats.

# Jarbidge Wilderness

With over 100 miles of hiking trails, Jarbidge Wilderness has a diverse landscape, including gorges that plummet thousands of feet to mountain ranges that seem to touch the sky. It's considered a must-see stop in Nevada and features a total of seven peaks. The most famous summit is Matterhorn Peak, which offers a 12-mile hike and reaches 10,389 feet. Fishing is permitted to give you a chance to catch bull trout and Dolly Varden as well as brown and rainbow trout. In the spring through the fall, there are 60 different varieties of wildflowers in the region.

**Best Time to Visit:** Jarbidge Wilderness is accessible all year round, but the area is at its peak in the spring and summer months.

**Pass/Permit/Fees:** It is free to enter Jarbidge Wilderness.

**Closest City or Town:** Jarbidge

**How to Get There:** From Jarbidge, head south on Main Street/NF-062 toward Bear Street N. Continue to follow NF-062 for 9.9 miles, then take a sharp right. Follow for 1.6 miles to the Jarbidge Mountains.

**GPS Coordinates:** 42.2914° N, -115.6111° W

**Did You Know?** Jarbidge was founded in 1909 when prospectors found gold in the region.

# Aliante Nature Discovery Park

Aliante Nature Discovery Park is a fantastic place for families. The park also has a waterfall and dinosaur park in addition to tennis and volleyball courts where kids can play. The dinosaur park also has a dino sandbox, so make sure to pack beach toys. There are bathrooms throughout the park, and most of the area is fenced in for safety and security. There is a walking park with wooden bridges spanning over creeks and lakes, which are great for photos. Within the dinosaur park, there are replicas of dinosaurs and hatchlings.

**Best Time to Visit:** Aliante Nature Discovery Park is open all year round, seven days a week.

**Pass/Permit/Fees:** It is free to enter Aliante Nature Discovery Park.

**Closest City or Town:** Las Vegas

**How to Get There:** From Las Vegas, take I-15 N to Exit 42A for Martin Luther King Boulevard. Merge onto US-95 N, heading toward Reno. Remain on US-95 N until you reach Exit 91A for Clark County Road 215. Keep right and merge onto Clark County Road 215 E. Take Exit 43 to merge onto N. Aliante Parkway. Continue to the destination at 2627 Nature Park Drive.

**GPS Coordinates:** 36.2868° N, -115.1759° W

**Did You Know?** If you are playing in the sandbox, you will find replicas of dinosaur bones. The sandbox simulates what it would be like to dig for fossils.

# Arrow Canyon Wilderness

Arrow Canyon Wilderness is 27,530 acres of beauty and wildlife. The canyon is home to Mojave yucca, barrel cactus, Joshua trees, and black brush. You may see bighorn sheep, desert tortoises, kit foxes, coyotes, bobcats, and lizards roaming the area. The area offers beautiful hikes and climbing to reach higher elevations. The range consists of a dark carbon layer underneath limestone. Arrow Canyon is so narrow and deep that the sun never reaches the bottom of the canyon in the winter months. There are several panoramic views of the canyon and surrounding area. You can camp in the canyon, and the park is an excellent place for stargazing at night.

**Best Time to Visit:** Arrow Canyon is accessible all year round.

**Pass/Permit/Fees:** It is free to enter the wilderness.

**Closest City or Town:** Las Vegas

**How to Get There:** From Las Vegas, get on I-515 N from N. 4$^{th}$ Street. Take Exit 76B to merge onto I-15 N toward Salt Lake City. Take Exit 64 for US-93 N toward Ely. Continue on US-93 N for 25.5 miles. Take a right. In 0.9 miles, take another right and follow for 3.7 miles to Arrow Canyon Wilderness.

**GPS Coordinates:** 36.6968° N, -114.8603° W

**Did You Know?** The highest elevations of the park range between 2,000 and 5,000 ft.

# Ash Meadows National Wildlife Refuge

Consisting of 23,000 acres, Ash Meadows National Wildlife Refuge is located in the Mojave Desert next to Death Valley. The area was deemed a refuge in 1971 and has been internationally studied in the field of wetland conservation. Its name is derived from the abundant ash trees in the area. Explorers wrote about them in their 1893 expedition notes, which influenced the name when the refuge was created in the summer of 1984 as a means of protecting the rare desert oasis. Ash Meadows National Wildlife Refuge is the home of Devil's Hole, a deep-water geothermal pool. The pool is so deep that the bottom has never been reached. All the water in the refuge is from the melted ice of the last ice age. The hole is home to the Devil's Hole pupfish, which is an endangered species.

**Best Time to Visit:** Ash Meadows National Wildlife Refuge is accessible all year round.

**Pass/Permit/Fees:** It is free to visit the refuge.

**Closest City or Town:** Las Vegas

**How to Get There:** From Las Vegas, get on I-515 N/US-95 N via N. 4th Street. Continue on US-95 N for 87.3 miles. Turn left onto NV-373 S, and follow for 14.5 miles. Turn left onto Spring Meadows Road, then continue for 3.4 miles to Ash Meadows National Wildlife Refuge.

**GPS Coordinates:** 36.4252° N, -116.3653° W

**Did You Know?** Ash Meadows is the largest oasis still in existence in the Mojave Desert.

## Bellagio Resort and Fountain Show

One of the most iconic Las Vegas resorts is the Italian-themed Bellagio Hotel and Casino. Unlike the Venetian, which only focuses on Venice, the Bellagio brings the best from all over Italy to Las Vegas. From Italian restaurants to a gelato stand to the famous Bellagio fountains, you will experience Italy's warm feel and hospitality. The fountains are the main tourist attraction. Every day from 8 a.m. to 3 p.m., the fountains perform every 30 minutes. From 8 p.m. to midnight, the fountains perform every 15 minutes. At night, the fountains are lit up in a dazzling show to the sound of popular tunes. Prepare for traffic stops on Las Vegas Boulevard as people pause to watch this wondrous delight.

**Best Time to Visit:** The Bellagio and fountain show is available all year round, seven days a week.

**Pass/Permit/Fees:** It is free to see the water show and enter the hotel and casino.

**Closest City or Town:** Las Vegas

**How to Get There:** The Bellagio Resort is on The Strip in Las Vegas. Its signature fountain is visible from the road. The address for the hotel is 3600 S. Las Vegas Boulevard.

**GPS Coordinates:** 36.1129° N, -115.1765° W

**Did You Know?** The Bellagio fountains and hotel were shooting locations for the 2001 Hollywood blockbuster *Ocean's Eleven.*

# Bowl of Fire

Bowl of Fire is a part of the Lake Mead National Recreation Area. The red, orange, and pink landscape is made of Aztec sandstone. The main hiking trail is considered moderate, and many who have hiked in this area say that it feels like you're on another planet—specifically, Mars. Because there are many caves and geological formations, there are opportunities for climbing and spelunking. Some trailheads require four-wheel drive to reach.

**Best Time to Visit:** Bowl of Fire is accessible all year round, but it's best to visit between October and April to avoid excessive heat.

**Pass/Permit/Fees:** You must pay to enter Lake Mead National Recreation Area. It costs $25 per vehicle.

**Closest City or Town:** Las Vegas

**How to Get There:** From Las Vegas, take a right onto E. Lake Mead Boulevard from Las Vegas Boulevard N. Turn left onto NV-167. Continue for 14.9 miles until you reach the Bowl of Fire trailhead. There are tolls on this route.

**GPS Coordinates:** 36.2264° N, -114.6700° W

**Did You Know?** Among the many rock formations you will see at Bowl of Fire, the most popular is Elephant Rock, which resembles an elephant and its trunk.

# Broadacres Marketplace and Event Center

Located in north Las Vegas, Broadacres Marketplace is a vast flea market with live entertainment. There are hundreds of vendors selling all sorts of goods and food. The space also has an events center for concerts. The variety of music played at the venue crosses over many genres and ranges from country music to Latin music to pop music.

**Best Time to Visit:** Broadacres Marketplace and Events Center is open all year; however, it is only open three days a week: Friday 4 p.m. to 11 p.m., Saturday 6 a.m. to 5 p.m., and Sunday 6 a.m. to 5 p.m.

**Pass/Permit/Fees:** Entering the marketplace costs $2.50 on Friday and Sunday and $1.50 on Saturday. Concert ticket prices vary, so check the website before attending.

**Closest City or Town:** Las Vegas

**How to Get There:** From the Las Vegas Strip, get on I-15 N. Take Exit 45 onto E. Lake Mead S Boulevard. Follow to Las Vegas Boulevard N, where you'll find the Broadacres Marketplace at 2930 Las Vegas Boulevard N.

**GPS Coordinates:** 36.2116° N, -115.1012° W

**Did You Know?** Broadacres Marketplace and Event Center was once a trailer park. It originally started in the 1970s as a swap meet. It is now one of the biggest flea markets in America.

# Cascata

Cascata is a luxurious golf course located outside of Las Vegas in Boulder City. The grounds are buried deep within the foothills of the River Mountains. The property offers breathtaking views, including a great view of Red Mountain, which stands at 3,600 feet. There are lakes and streams throughout the property that you will see while golfing on the par-72 course. There is also an event space for meetings, gatherings, and weddings.

**Best Time to Visit:** Cascata is open year round.

**Pass/Permit/Fees:** It is free to enter the golf course, but fees apply to play golf, become a member, or eat in the restaurant.

**Closest City or Town:** Las Vegas

**How to Get There:** From Las Vegas, take I-515 S. Follow I-515 S until it turns into I-1 S. Take Exit 15B for US-93. Take US-95 S ramp to Searchlight/Needles. Keep left at the fork, then take another left onto NV-173. That will become Cascata Drive, where you will find the golf course at 1 Cascata Drive.

**GPS Coordinates:** 35.9739° N, -114.8955° W

**Did You Know?** *Cascata* is the Italian word for waterfall, which is appropriate considering there is a 418-foot-tall waterfall on the property that crashes down into a mile-long stream. The buildings are designed to resemble Tuscany.

# Caesar's Palace and the Colosseum

Caesar's Palace and The Colosseum are two of the most visited spots on the Las Vegas Strip. The hotel and casino feature Roman and Greek architecture. The hotel has a mall and restaurant area that is designed to look like Ancient Rome. When you enter the casino, there are giant statues throughout the hotel. The Colosseum is the concert venue that houses artists in residence. Some of the famous singers that have resided at the Colosseum include Cher, Celine Dion, Lady Gaga, and Bette Midler.

**Best Time to Visit:** Caesar's Palace is open year round.

**Pass/Permit/Fees:** It is free to enter the hotel and casino, but you must pay for tickets for the shows at the Colosseum.

**Closest City or Town:** Las Vegas

**How to Get There:** Caesar's Palace can be found on the central Las Vegas Strip at 3570 Las Vegas Boulevard S.

**GPS Coordinates:** 36.1162° N, -115.1745° W

**Did You Know?** A massive statue of Augustus Ceasar guards the hotel property. The hotel and casino were inspired by the Roman emperor Nero, who was known for his wild parties and debauchery. The hotel has been renovated seven times and has been featured in over 20 Hollywood films.

# City View Park

Located in north Las Vegas, City View Park is a popular destination for locals to relax, play, and gather with family and friends. The park offers many amenities, though the picnic areas are especially popular. You can get a group picnic area for large gatherings or an individual picnic area for a smaller group of people.

While in the park, you can play horseshoes or use the two playgrounds. The most beautiful part of the park is a waterfall that crashes down into a stream that meanders through the park and eventually ends in a pond.

**Best Time to Visit:** City View Park is open and available all year round.

**Pass/Permit/Fees:** It is free to enjoy City View Park.

**Closest City or Town:** Las Vegas

**How to Get There:** From Las Vegas, take I-15 N to Exit 46 for Cheyenne Avenue. Turn left onto E. Cheyenne Avenue, and you will see the entrance to the park on the left at 101 E. Cheyenne Avenue.

**GPS Coordinates:** 36.2169° N, -115.1361° W

**Did You Know?** Throughout the year, the pond at City View Park hosts fishing derbies.

# Clark County Heritage Museum

Located in Henderson, the Clark County Heritage Museum has collections and artifacts that revolve around the discovery and history of southern Nevada. Many of the exhibits focus on the first Native Americans—the Paiute tribe—and their way of life. Other items and exhibits chronicle the mining industry, the railroad, and the history of gaming in the state. A lot of the artifacts found in the museum were donated by Edith Roberts, whose mother was a mortician who traveled around southern Nevada. During her travels, she amassed a considerable collection of items and stored them in Las Vegas.

**Best Time to Visit:** The Clark County Heritage Museum is open year round except for major holidays.

**Pass/Permit/Fees:** Adults cost $2, while seniors and children cost $1 each to enter the museum.

**Closest City or Town:** Las Vegas

**How to Get There:** From Las Vegas, take I-515 until it turns into I-11 S. Take Exit 17 for Wagonwheel Drive. Take a left onto NV-582 and a right onto Museum Drive. Turn left onto Sausalito Drive and then right back onto Museum Drive to reach Clark County Heritage Museum at 1830 S. Boulder Highway.

**GPS Coordinates:** 36.0102° N, -114.9454° W

**Did You Know?** The museum has built a replica of a mining ghost town.

# Cowabunga Bay Water Park

Cowabunga Bay Water Park is located in Henderson, just outside of Las Vegas. The water park is massive, with dozens of waterslides and pools. There are twists and turns and miles of slides for kids and adults to enjoy. The park opened in 2015 and is one of the most popular destinations in southern Nevada. It is the perfect way to cool off from the desert heat. Aside from the water park and swimming pools, you can also rent cabanas for the day to get some shade and relax from your adventures. Cowabunga Bay is a great family activity that everyone will love.

**Best Time to Visit:** Cowabunga Bay Water Park is best in the summer.

**Pass/Permit/Fees:** General admission to Cowabunga Bay is $42.95. Children under 4 feet tall cost $29.95. Parking costs $8. Cabana rentals range from $180 to $250.

**Closest City or Town:** Las Vegas

**How to Get There:** From Las Vegas, take I-515 S to Exit 64B for Galleria Drive. Make a left, and you will see the water park at 900 Galleria Drive.

**GPS Coordinates:** 36.0722° N, -115.0252° W

**Did You Know?** Cowabunga Bay has a waterslide that is entirely in the dark. At various times, it lights up with different displays.

# Death Valley National Park

Death Valley is the lowest geographical location in America. It has the highest summer temperatures in the nation, reaching over 120°F. The park was established in the 1990s and is known for its colorful rocks and canyon.

Chloride City is a ghost town nestled in Death Valley. The city was established in the early 1900s as a mining town. The settlement only lasted one year before it was abandoned entirely. Chloride City is one of many ghost towns in the area.

**Best Time to Visit:** Death Valley is best visited in the winter months when the weather is not extremely hot. It is best to visit from October through March.

**Pass/Permit/Fees:** It costs $30 to enter Death Valley National Park.

**Closest City or Town:** Las Vegas

**How to Get There:** From Las Vegas, get on I-515 N from N. 4th Street. Merge onto I-515 N/US-95 N. Stay on US-95 N for about 117 miles. Turn left onto NV-374 S. Follow for 8.9 miles until you reach Death Valley, National Park.

**GPS Coordinates:** 36.5054° N, -117.0794° W

**Did You Know?** Death Valley is the home of the Moving Rocks, which mysteriously drag across the playa or dry lake, leaving marks in the sand. Researchers believe a combination of wind and ice may cause these rocks to move from time to time.

# Eldorado Wilderness

Eldorado Wilderness is 32,016 acres of natural land. The mountains of the wilderness were formed 15 million years ago during a volcanic explosion. The area of Eldorado was founded during the gold rush. The name Eldorado came from the abundance of gold found in the area. There are several canyons for exploration, and the park also sits on the Colorado River. The landscape is composed of red, brown, and white metamorphic rock. There are several ridges and peaks throughout the wilderness that were formed over millions of years by rivers, washes, and drainages. The peaks rise 500 to 1,200 feet above the Colorado River.

**Best Time to Visit:** Eldorado Wilderness is open all year.

**Pass/Permit/Fees:** It is free to enter Eldorado Wilderness.

**Closest City or Town:** Las Vegas

**How to Get There:** From Las Vegas, head northeast on Las Vegas Boulevard N toward E. Ogden Avenue. Turn right to merge onto I-515 S. Follow I-515 S to NV-165 E in Boulder City. From I-515 S, continue onto I-11 S. Take Exit 14 to merge onto US-95 S toward Searchlight. Turn left onto NV-165 E. In 13.5 miles, take another left. In 0.3 miles, merge onto Nelson Cutoff Road. In 0.6 miles, turn right onto Eldorado Wilderness Road.

**GPS Coordinates:** 35.7652° N, -114.7790° W

**Did You Know?** The rocky, craggy landscape of Eldorado Wilderness was formed during the Miocene Basin uplift.

# Excalibur Hotel

The Excalibur Hotel in Las Vegas is a popular themed hotel and casino on the Las Vegas Strip. The Excalibur Hotel is named after the famous sword from the classic tale of King Arthur. The medieval-themed hotel is shaped like a castle surrounded by a moat. One of the more popular shows is called Feast of Kings. It is a traditional medieval jousting show where knights on horseback fight each other to a fictional death. The hotel is on a list of the top castles in America.

**Best Time to Visit:** The Excalibur Hotel is open all year round.

**Pass/Permit/Fees:** It is free to enter the hotel and casino; however, ticket prices vary for any shows.

**Closest City or Town:** Las Vegas

**How to Get There:** The hotel is located on the Southern end of the Las Vegas Strip at 3850 S. Las Vegas Boulevard.

**GPS Coordinates:** 36.0989° N, -115.1753° W

**Did You Know?** Until 2007, there was a life-sized statue of Merlin the Magician overlooking the resort from a high turret in the castle.

# Flightlinez Bootleg Canyon

Flightlinez Bootleg Canyon is a zipline park in Boulder City located just outside of Las Vegas. Flightlinez Bootleg Canyon is on Red Mountain. You will zip line down one of four different lines for the 1.5-mile ride back to the bottom. Zipline tours are available during the day, sunset, or even at night, granting you the best views of the canyon.

A safety class is required beforehand, and qualified instructors guide all tours to ensure an accident-free, fun time.

**Best Time to Visit:** Flightlinez Bootleg Canyon is usually open all year round; however, it is best to check the website for temporary closures before visiting.

**Pass/Permit/Fees:** Depending on which tour you decide to take, Flightlinez tours range between $135–$159.

**Closest City or Town:** Las Vegas

**How to Get There:** From Las Vegas, take I-515 S. I-515 S will turn into I-11 S. Continue until you reach Exit 15B for Business/Boulder City Parkway. After a few miles, you will see the entrance to Flightlinez Bootleg Canyon at 1644 Boulder City Parkway.

**GPS Coordinates:** 35.9695° N, -114.8578° W

**Did You Know?** The top of Red Mountain reaches 3,800 feet.

# Floyd Lamb Park

Floyd Lamb Park is a 680-acre park known for its wildlife, vegetation, and scenic views of the Spring Mountain and Sheep Mountain ranges. It is a common refreshing respite for the residents of Las Vegas. Located on Tule Springs, a collection of small lakes, you'll find four ponds popular for fishing, an archaeological site, a wash, and the Tule Springs Ranch.

Tule Springs Ranch offers an educational experience about the traditional style of working as a rancher, early ranching life in Nevada, and the overall way of life in Las Vegas.

**Best Time to Visit:** Floyd Lamb Park is open all year round.

**Pass/Permit/Fees:** It is free to enter Floyd Lamb Park.

**Closest City or Town:** Las Vegas

**How to Get There:** From Las Vegas, take I-515 N to US-95 N. Take Exit 93, and turn right onto N. Durango Drive. Take another right onto Brent Lane. You'll find Floyd Lamb Park on 9200 Tule Springs Road.

**GPS Coordinates:** 36.3228° N, -115.2680° W

**Did You Know?** Floyd Lamb Park is a desert oasis in the Mohave Desert. The park was named after Floyd Lamb, a Democratic senator for Nevada who served from 1956–1983.

# Fremont Street Experience

The Fremont Street Experience is located in Las Vegas. Fremont Street is the location of the original Las Vegas Hotels. Once a regular street you could drive down and park on, Fremont Street has since closed down to traffic and served as a pedestrian walkway where visitors can walk into the street, sit, hang out, and enjoy drinks and food. A vast cover stretched over the road lights up and has a screen showing various colors and images for the people sitting outside. Underneath the cover, there is a nightly light show. Ziplining is available at Slotzilla Zipline, and stages for outdoor concerts dot the avenue. Fremont Street draws many Las Vegas residents and visitors in with its lively scene.

**Best Time to Visit:** Fremont Street is open to the public year round.

**Pass/Permit/Fees:** It is free to walk down Fremont Street and enter the casinos.

**Closest City or Town:** Las Vegas

**How to Get There:** From the Las Vegas Strip, drive north on S. Las Vegas Boulevard until you reach Fremont Street.

**GPS Coordinates:** 36.1558° N, -115.1178° W

**Did You Know?** Fremont Street was the original Las Vegas Strip. It is home to the Golden Nugget, the D, the 4 Queens, Main Street, and Binion's. It has been featured in a lot of movies.

# Gold Butte National Monument

Gold Butte National Monument is just outside of the Grand Canyon-Parashant National Monument in the southeastern region of Nevada. As part of the Mojave Desert, the barren desert land is home to many beautiful rock formations and caves.

In the early 1900s, Gold Butte was a mining site. There are still remnants of its history hidden amongst the landscape. While on your hikes, you will see tons of Joshua trees, and you may even see goats in the "21 Goats" area.

**Best Time to Visit:** Gold Butte National Monument is accessible all year round, but spring and fall are ideal for hiking to avoid the intense summer heat.

**Pass/Permit/Fees:** It is free to enter Gold Butte National Monument.

**Closest City or Town:** Las Vegas

**How to Get There:** From Las Vegas, get on I-515 N from N. 4th Street. Follow I-15 N to Mesquite. Take Exit 112 from I-15 N. Follow for 69.9 miles until you reach Gold Butte Road.

**GPS Coordinates:** 36.3778° N, -114.1652° W

**Did You Know?** As you hike through Gold Butte National Monument, you will see ancient drawings on the walls of the rocks. These drawings go back to the days of early Native Americans and illustrate how they may have survived in the desert.

## Golden Nugget Casino Resort

The Golden Nugget Casino Resort is one of the original casinos in Las Vegas. The hotel is steeped in Las Vegas gaming history. Opened in 1946 when gaming started making its way to Las Vegas, the hotel is located on historic Fremont Street.

The Golden Nugget has been featured in many Las Vegas movies, including *Next*, *Smokin' Aces*, *The Grand*, and the famous Elvis Presley movie *Viva Las Vegas*. It also appeared in the Bee Gee's iconic disco music video for "Night Fever."

**Best Time to Visit:** The Golden Nugget is open and accessible all year round.

**Pass/Permit/Fees:** It is free to enter the hotel and casino.

**Closest City or Town:** Las Vegas

**How to Get There:** From S. Las Vegas Boulevard, go north until you come to Fremont Street. You will find the casino along the promenade at 129 Fremont Street.

**GPS Coordinates:** 36.1700° N, -115.1450° W

**Did You Know?** The world's largest gold nugget, "The Hand of Faith," is on display in the lobby of the Golden Nugget. The nugget weighs 60 pounds and is 18 inches in length. Discovered in Australia, the nugget has been on display at the casino since 1981.

# Grapevine Canyon

Grapevine Canyon is part of Spirit Canyon Wilderness, Lake Mead National Recreation Area, and Bridge Canyon Wilderness Area in the southeastern part of Nevada.

The canyon has lots of hiking, with the Grapevine Canyon Trail as the most popular to hike. Native American petroglyphs cover much of Grapevine Canyon, granting a glimpse into ancient life. There is also a shallow ravine that runs through the Newberry Mountains. The gorge offers water to the plants and animals but is not safe to drink.

**Best Time to Visit:** Grapevine Canyon is accessible all year round.

**Pass/Permit/Fees:** It is free to enjoy Grapevine Canyon.

**Closest City or Town:** Las Vegas

**How to Get There:** From Las Vegas, get on I-515 S. Continue on I-515 S. Take US-95 to NV-163 E for 76.3 miles. Continue onto NV-163 E. Drive to Christmas Tree Pass Road.

**GPS Coordinates:** 35.2311° N, -114.6793° W

**Did You Know?** You will see cottonwood, arrow weed, and canyon grape growing throughout the canyon. Finches, bighorn sheep, bobcats, and lizards are common animals to spot while hiking.

# Hemenway Valley Park

Located in Boulder City, Hemenway Valley Park is one of the most popular parks in the city. Located next to Lake Mead, you can get a great view of the lake while spending time with friends and family. The park offers a lot of outdoor activities and sports.

While in the park, you will find two lighted tennis courts so that you can play day or night. There are also two lighted softball fields. Other amenities include basketball courts, horseshoes, and playgrounds. There are several picnic areas for families and friends to gather and celebrate.

**Best Time to Visit:** Hemenway Valley Park is accessible all year round.

**Pass/Permit/Fees:** It is free to enter the park.

**Closest City or Town:** Las Vegas

**How to Get There:** From Las Vegas, take I-515 S, which will turn into I-11 S. From I-11 S, take Exit 15B for US-93 Business/Boulder City Parkway. Turn left onto Ville Drive. Take a right onto Key Largo Drive, and Hemenway Park will be on your left at 401 Ville Drive.

**GPS Coordinates:** 35.9952° N, -114.8321° W

**Did You Know?** The most popular sight in the park is the bighorn sheep. Park-goers can see several sheep as they come down from the hills to graze in the park.

## Henderson Bird Viewing Preserve

The Henderson Bird Viewing Preserve is a respite for desert birds and waterfowl. The 0.75-mile trail is paved or has soft surfaces that are wheelchair accessible. There are nine ponds in the preserve where birds come to bathe and drink.

Located on the edge of the Pacific Migratory Flyway, most of the birds are temporary. Visitors are asked to not feed the birds because it may disrupt their interactions with other birds in the wild. Visitors are able to rent binoculars if you don't have your own.

**Best Time to Visit:** Henderson Bird Viewing Preserve is accessible all year round.

**Pass/Permit/Fees:** It is free to enter the preserve.

**Closest City or Town:** Las Vegas

**How to Get There:** From Las Vegas, take I-515 S to Exit 64B for Galleria Drive. Make a left onto N. Moser Drive. After 400 feet, make a right, and the preserve is on the left at 350 E. Galleria Drive.

**GPS Coordinates:** 36.0711° N, -115.0011° W

**Did You Know?** Tino the Tortoise lives in the preserve. He hibernates from October to March, so try to meet him in the warmer weather months.

## High Roller Ferris Wheel

Located on the Las Vegas Strip, the High Roller Ferris Wheel is 550 feet tall and doubles as an observation wheel, allowing visitors to see sky-high views of Las Vegas and all the hotels and casinos. It takes 30 minutes for the wheel to make one revolution.

The 28 cabins that make up the Ferris wheel are spacious and can hold up to ten people. There is a happy hour opportunity where you can hire a bartender to serve drinks to you and your friends while you make the revolution around the wheel.

**Best Time to Visit:** The High Roller Ferris Wheel is available all year round.

**Pass/Permit/Fees:** There are day prices and night prices to ride the High Roller Ferris Wheel. Day prices: $23.50 for adults and $8.50 for children. Night prices: $34.75 for adults and $17.50 for children. Happy hour is $60.

**Closest City or Town:** Las Vegas

**How to Get There:** The Ferris wheel is located at the Linq Promenade on the central Las Vegas Strip.

**GPS Coordinates:** 36.1176° N, -115.1683° W

**Did You Know?** The High Roller is the world's tallest observation wheel.

# Hoover Dam

The Hoover Dam is an architectural wonder on the Colorado River. It is located in the Black Canyon on the border between Nevada and Arizona. Lake Mead is not a natural lake but rather the largest reservoir in the world, created from damming the Colorado River. It has become one of the most popular recreation areas in America.

Built during the Great Depression, the dam was dedicated by then-president Franklin D. Roosevelt. Originally named the Boulder Dam, it was changed to bear the name of President Herbert Hoover. About 100 men lost their lives building the dam.

**Best Time to Visit:** Hoover Dam is open and accessible all year round.

**Pass/Permit/Fees:** Tour tickets of the dam range from $10 to $30, depending on what kind of experience you choose.

**Closest City or Town:** Las Vegas

**How to Get There:** From Las Vegas, take US-93 S to Exit 2. After exiting, make a U-turn at the roundabout and get onto NV-172. Follow the road to the Hoover Dam.

**GPS Coordinates:** 36.0161° N, -114.7377° W

**Did You Know?** You used to be able to drive over Hoover Dam. Although NV-93 goes over the dam, a bypass was created down the highway to give an alternate path over the Colorado River due to structural concerns.

## Lake Mead National Conservation Area

Lake Mead is a reservoir formed when the Hoover Dam was built on the Colorado River. The area is 247.1 square miles, and the lake has a volume of 7.735 cubic miles.

The lake is ideal for swimming, biking, boating, and fishing. Lake Mead offers a lot of hiking and camping opportunities. Hiking trails can take you up to the highest points in the park, with great views of Lake Mead and Lake Mohave.

**Best Time to Visit:** Lake Mead National Conservation area is accessible all year round.

**Pass/Permit/Fees:** It costs $25 to enter Lake Mead.

**Closest City or Town:** Las Vegas

**How to Get There:** From Las Vegas, follow I-515 S to W. Galleria Drive in Henderson. Take Exit 64B and I-515 S. Continue for 10.7 miles. Follow W. Galleria Drive for 9.4 miles to E. Lake Mead Parkway. The lake is relatively large, so check GPS coordinates and take a map along with you. There are also tolls along this route.

**GPS Coordinates:** 36.1435° N, -114.4144° W

**Did You Know?** Designated as the nation's first recreational area, Lake Mead has a little bit of something for everyone.

# Las Vegas Distillery

The Las Vegas Distillery, located in Henderson, is the only distillery built in Nevada since the end of Prohibition in 1933. It took some time for the distillery to get its license and fully open, but now it is a popular spot for those who enjoy spirits. The distillery has a full tasting room and offers whiskey, vodka, gin, rum, and moonshine. Everything is distilled in two copper pot stills known as the "Copper Angels." Full barrels and casks are available for purchase so that you can have your own authentic barrel in your home.

**Best Time to Visit:** The distillery is open all year round.

**Pass/Permit/Fees:** It costs $15 to either take a tour or participate in a tasting. It costs $25 to do both. Whiskey barrels range from $200–$250 each. Of course, you must be 21 years of age to enter.

**Closest City or Town:** Las Vegas

**How to Get There:** From Las Vegas, take I-515 S to Auto Show Drive in Henderson at Exit 62. Take Auto Drive Road to Eastgate Road, where you will find the distillery.

**GPS Coordinates:** 36.0547° N, -115.0192° W

**Did You Know?** The distillery opened on April 1, 2011, exactly 100 years after the founding of Las Vegas.

## Las Vegas Motor Speedway

The Las Vegas Motor Speedway, known initially as the Speedrome, opened in 1972 as a drag strip and speedway. Over time, the Speedrome went from a 3/8-of-a-mile loop in 1985 to a 1.5-mile loop in 1996. It has since grown to host NASCAR events and has become one of the top raceways in the country. The venue holds 80,000 people and offers campgrounds for RVs. The speedway was built after the closure of the Stardust International Raceway in 1971.

**Best Time to Visit:** The speedway is available all year round during events.

**Pass/Permit/Fees:** The price of each event differs, but tickets must be purchased to enter.

**Closest City or Town:** Las Vegas

**How to Get There:** The address is 7000 Las Vegas Boulevard N. The speedway is on the city's outskirts. To get there from the Strip, take I-15 N to Speedway Boulevard at Exit 54. Follow Speedway Boulevard to Checkered Flag Lane, where you will find the entrance to the speedway.

**GPS Coordinates:** 36.2723° N, -115.0103° W

**Did You Know?** On October 16, 2011, there was a fatal 15-car crash on the track during the final race of the 2011 IndyCar season. Due to one of the drivers dying, the race was never completed, and IndyCar has stopped racing at the Speedway.

## Lion Habitat Ranch

The Lion Habitat Ranch is located in Henderson, just outside of Las Vegas. It is home to several lions, a giraffe, and wild birds. The ranch was opened in 1989 and has served as a refuge ever since. The proceeds from ticket sales and donations all go to keeping wild lion habitats open around the world. The habitat offers events and tours of the grounds where you can meet and feed the animals. The ranchers believe that guests feeding the animals creates a bond and helps provide a loving environment for the lions.

**Best Time to Visit:** The Lion Habitat Ranch is open all year round.

**Pass/Permit/Fees:** To enter the ranch, it costs $25 if you are an out-of-state resident and $20 for Nevada locals. Children under the age of 4 are free, and children ages 4–14 are free with the purchase of one adult ticket. There are discounts for seniors, military personnel, and hotel employees.

**Closest City or Town:** Las Vegas

**How to Get There:** From Las Vegas, take I-15 S to Exit 27, then get on St. Rose Parkway. From St. Rose Parkway, turn onto Bruner Avenue, and you will see the habitat.

**GPS Coordinates:** 35.9701° N, -115.1555° W

**Did You Know?** At the ranch, you can meet Ozzie, the painting giraffe. You can stand by him as he creates his next masterpiece.

# Luxor Hotel

The Luxor Hotel is a popular themed hotel on the Las Vegas Strip. Designed after one of the Pyramids of Giza, the hotel has décor that encapsulates sarcophagi, renderings of Nefertiti and King Tut, and hieroglyphics.

In the hotel, you'll find the Aurora bar, which is named after the northern lights. It is one of the most famous hotel bars in the city, where the ceiling is lit up to resemble its namesake. Other small casino bars found throughout the hotel offer drinks, video poker, and social mingling. Like all the Vegas hotels, there is a pool area and casino along with shops and restaurants.

**Best Time to Visit:** The Luxor is open all year round.

**Pass/Permit/Fees:** Entering the hotel or casino is free.

**Closest City or Town:** Las Vegas

**How to Get There:** The address of the hotel is 3900 S. Las Vegas Boulevard. It is located on the main Las Vegas Strip.

**GPS Coordinates:** 36.0955° N, -115.1761° W

**Did You Know?** The top of the Luxor Pyramid has a huge spotlight that shines up into the night sky. The light is so bright that it can be seen from space.

# Madame Tussaud's

Madame Tussaud's brand was named after famous French wax artist Marie Tussaud. The museum first opened in 1835. There are now several locations around the globe. At the Las Vegas location, the wax museum offers many interactive experiences. The most popular one is a *Hangover*-themed bar named after the famous Hollywood movie. There are several wax figures of the movie's stars for you to sit around and have cocktails with. There is also a wrecking ball room where you can take a picture alongside Miley Cyrus and another area where you can make a music video with a wax replica of Drake. There is even a Marvel Universe room.

**Best Time to Visit:** Madame Tussaud's is open all year round.

**Pass/Permit/Fees:** Madame Tussaud's offers several packages and experiences at the museum that range in price from $37 for general admission up to $85 for admission, photo passes, and access to certain exhibits.

**Closest City or Town:** Las Vegas

**How to Get There:** The address for Madame Tussaud's is 3377 S. Las Vegas Boulevard, located on the Strip.

**GPS Coordinates:** 36.1213° N, -115.1711° W

**Did You Know?** Madame Tussaud was once scheduled for execution, but she was released and fled to Great Britain, where she toured her work and eventually opened her museum.

# Mandalay Bay and the Shark Reef Aquarium

The Shark Reef Aquarium at Mandalay Bay is one of the largest aquariums in the United States. Its main tank holds 1.3 million gallons of water. While walking through the aquarium and its two underwater tunnels, you will come face to face with around 2,000 different sea creatures, including sea turtles, jellyfish, stingrays, golden crocodiles, piranhas, and sharks. There are over 100 sharks, and 30 of them live in the massive main tank. Exhibits have featured coral reefs, the Caribbean Ocean, and Burmese pythons. You will also have access to the Mandalay Bay casino, restaurants, and shops.

**Best Time to Visit:** The aquarium is open all year round.

**Pass/Permit/Fees:** It costs $21 to enter the aquarium.

**Closest City or Town:** Las Vegas

**How to Get There:** The aquarium is part of the Mandalay Hotel and Casino, which is relatively close to Las Vegas's McCarran International Airport. The address of the aquarium is 3950 S. Las Vegas Boulevard.

**GPS Coordinates:** 36.0888° N, -115.1765° W

**Did You Know?** Many gamblers are referred to as "sharks." Card players in particular are typically called "card sharks."

# Mary Jane Falls Trail

The Mary Jane Falls Trail is 2.5 miles long and located in the Mount Charleston Wilderness. The path starts next to a long-forgotten road that wraps around boulders placed on the trail to help preserve it by shielding it from erosion. At the trail's end, the falls flow all year round and are fed by natural springs. Dogs are allowed to use this trail, but they must be kept on a leash. It can get a bit rocky, so make sure you wear sturdy shoes with great ankle support. Parts of the trail can get a bit tough as you go up the incline.

**Best Time to Visit:** Accessible all year round, Mary Jane Falls Trail is best from April through October. Because there is a heavy flow of traffic on the trail, it is best to go early to avoid the crowds.

**Pass/Permit/Fees:** It is free to enter Mount Charleston Wilderness.

**Closest City or Town:** Las Vegas

**How to Get There:** From Las Vegas, follow US-95 N and NV-157 to Echo Road/Kyle Canyon Road in Mount Charleston. Follow for 38.2 miles, and continue onto Echo Road Drive to reach Mary Jane Big Falls Road.

**GPS Coordinates:** 36.2672° N, -115.6624° W

**Did You Know?** You will see trees like sagebrush, alpine, aspen, and bristlecone. Wildflowers in the area include monkeyflowers, lupines, paintbrushes, and buckwheat.

# Meadow Valley Range Wilderness

Located in eastern Nevada, Meadow Valley Range Wilderness is 123,488 acres of high ranges and deep canyon valleys. It is home to several species of wildlife and plant life. It's a good place for camping, hiking, rock climbing, and backpacking.

Sunflower Mountain is the most popular spot to visit while in Meadow Valley Range Wilderness. From the top of the peak, visitors will find breathtaking views of the entire area. A wide variety of trees grow along the trails. Mule deer, bobcats, mountain lions, lizards, and rattlesnakes are common wildlife to spot while exploring.

**Best Time to Visit:** Meadow Valley Range Wilderness is accessible all year round.

**Pass/Permit/Fees:** It is free to enter Meadow Valley Range Wilderness.

**Closest City or Town:** Las Vegas

**How to Get There:** From Las Vegas, get on I-515 N. Follow I-15 N and US-93 N to Kane Springs Road in Alamo. Continue on Kane Springs Road for 15.5 miles until you reach Meadow Valley Range Wilderness.

**GPS Coordinates:** 37.0760° N, -114.7309° W

**Did You Know?** The state of Nevada is considering building a large city in Coyote Springs Valley that could become Nevada's third-largest city.

# Mike O'Callaghan-Pat Tillman Memorial Bridge

The Mike O'Callaghan-Pat Tillman Memorial Bridge spans the Colorado River about 30 miles outside of Las Vegas. The bridge is part of I-11 and State Highway 93, connecting Nevada and Arizona. The original State Highway 93 used to go over the Hoover Dam. After many years, officials determined that the road was not safe to travel on because of tight turns and blind spots, so the new route was planned out, and the bridge was built between 2003 and 2010. The bridge officially opened on October 19, 2010. It's jointly named after 1970s-era Nevada governors Mike O'Callaghan and Pat Tillman.

**Best Time to Visit:** The Mike O'Callaghan-Pat Tillman Memorial Bridge is opened all year round.

**Pass/Permit/Fees:** There are no tolls to cross the bridge.

**Closest City or Town:** Las Vegas

**How to Get There:** From Las Vegas, take State Highway 93 S to the bridge. You can also take I-515 S to I-11 S.

**GPS Coordinates:** 36.0125° N, -114.7414° W

**Did You Know?** The Mike O'Callaghan-Pat Tillman Bridge has the widest concrete arch in the western hemisphere and the tallest in the world. It is also the second-highest bridge in America, standing at 890 feet.

# Mirage Hotel and Casino

The Mirage Hotel and Casino is known as the home of the famous Siegfried & Roy. The duo was most famous for their long-standing show of doing tricks with large animals, specifically tigers, and lions. Their legacy continues with the Secret Garden and Dolphin Habitat. The Secret Garden is a place for some of the rarest big cats in the world, like white striped tigers, snow-white tigers, white lions, and leopards. The animals live in lush surroundings with waterfalls as they hunt and watch after their prides. The Mirage Hotel also features the Erupting Volcano. The volcano only erupts four times a day, on the hour, between the hours of 8 p.m. and 11 p.m. The volcano erupts just outside of the hotel on Las Vegas Boulevard.

**Best Time to Visit:** The Secret Garden and the Erupting Volcano are open all year round.

**Pass/Permit/Fees:** It is free to watch the volcano erupt, but admission to Siegfried & Roy's Secret Garden costs $25.

**Closest City or Town:** Las Vegas

**How to Get There:** The address for the Mirage Hotel is 3400 S. Las Vegas Boulevard, located on the Strip.

**GPS Coordinates:** 36.1212° N, -115.1741° W

**Did You Know?** On his birthday, October 3, 2003, Roy Horn was severely injured by one of the tigers during a live show. The act was discontinued immediately.

# Mount Charleston

Mount Charleston is located in the Spring Mountain National Recreation Area just outside of Las Vegas. It is an ideal location for hiking, backpacking, mountain climbing, picnicking, and camping. Dogs are allowed on certain hiking trails in the park. The mountain also offers science safaris, art workshops, and night hikes.

**Best Time to Visit:** Mount Charleston is accessible all year round, but spring and fall ideal for adventuring.

**Pass/Permit/Fees:** If you are a Nevada resident, it is $10 to enter Spring Mountain National Recreation Area. If you are a non-Nevada resident, it is $15.

**Closest City or Town:** Las Vegas

**How to Get There:** From Las Vegas, head northeast on Las Vegas Boulevard N toward E. Ogden Avenue. Turn left at the first cross street onto E. Ogden Avenue. Turn right in 387 feet onto N. 4$^{th}$ Street. Use any lane to merge onto I-515 N/US-95 N via the ramp to I-15 N. Continue onto US-95 N. Keep on US-95 N until you reach Exit 96. Take Exit 96 toward NV-157 W/Kyle Canyon Road. Continue onto NV-157 W for 16.4 miles. At the traffic circle, take the second exit onto NV-157 W. Stay on NV-157 W, and Mount Charleston Wilderness will be on the right.

**GPS Coordinates:** 36.2572° N, -115.6426° W

**Did You Know?** Mount Charleston is home to the first national Cold War memorial.

# Mouse's Tank

Mouse's Tank is part of the famous Valley of Fire. It is a natural basin, and after each rainfall, water collects at the bottom. It gets its name from the Southern Paiute Native American Tribe renegade known as "Little Mouse." Accused of killing two prospectors, among other crimes, he was forced to hide out in the basin.

Several hiking trails in the region are moderately easy and take about 20–30 minutes to complete. There are parking areas, restrooms, and picnic spots near Mouse's Tank.

**Best Time to Visit:** Mouse's Tank is accessible all year round.

**Pass/Permit/Fees:** It is $10 to enter the Valley of Fire. It costs $20 to camp.

**Closest City or Town:** Las Vegas

**How to Get There:** From Las Vegas, get on I-515 N/US-95 N from N. 4th St. Follow I-15 N, then take Exit 75 and drive for 33.3 miles. Continue on Valley of Fire Highway. Drive to Mouse's Tank Road/White Domes Road. This is a remote location; check GPS and keep a map on you.

**GPS Coordinates:** 36.4378° N, -114.5123° W

**Did You Know?** Over 100 million years ago, the area that is Mouse's Tank was a massive sea. When the water receded over time, it became the natural phenomenon that it is today. The water gave way to Aztec sandstone.

# Neon Museum

Las Vegas is known for its neon lights. The Neon Museum's mission is to preserve and study Las Vegas's historic neon signs. Dubbed the "Neon Boneyard," you will see signs from all the former Vegas hotels that are no longer standing. The museum also offers an artist's residency where selected artists can create pieces in a visual medium inspired by the neon work on display.

**Best Time to Visit:** The Neon Museum is open all year round between the hours of 3 p.m. and 11 p.m.

**Pass/Permit/Fees:** General admission is $20 for non-locals and $16 for locals. This includes a 1-hour tour between 3 p.m. and 6 p.m. Guided tours are from 7 p.m. until 10:45 p.m. and cost $28 for non-locals and $24 for locals. An in-house exhibition entitled *Brilliant!* is available outside from 9 p.m. to 11 p.m. and costs $23 for non-locals and $19 for locals. If you have a membership, everything is free.

**Closest City or Town:** Las Vegas

**How to Get There:** In Las Vegas, you can find the museum at 770 N. Las Vegas Boulevard at the end of the Strip.

**GPS Coordinates:** 36.1770° N, -115.1353° W

**Did You Know?** The most famous sign in the museum is from the former Stardust Hotel that hosted the Rat Pack.

## Nevada State Museum, Las Vegas

With seven locations throughout the state, the Nevada State Museum in Las Vegas is dedicated to preserving Nevada's history. The museum offers interactive experiences for its visitors. The exhibits revolve around the geology of Las Vegas as well as the building of the luxurious city. The more scientific exhibits contain fossils found in Nevada from prehistoric times and explore the animals and plants found in Nevada. There is also a botanical garden and springs preserve. The preserve is 180 acres of nature walks and installations for all to enjoy.

**Best Time to Visit:** The museum is available all year round, Wednesday through Friday. Non-members must make a reservation.

**Pass/Permit/Fees:** Adults cost $9.95, and children over the age of 3 cost $4.95.

**Closest City or Town:** Las Vegas

**How to Get There:** From the strip, take I-15 N to US-95 N. Take the Valley View Boulevard exit, and at Meadow Lane, you will see the museum at 309 S. Valley View Boulevard.

**GPS Coordinates:** 36.1722° N, -115.1901° W

**Did You Know?** You can also take virtual tours of the museum from home or school. The virtual tour comes with study questions and a quiz.

# New York, New York Hotel and Casino

The New York, New York Hotel and Casino in Las Vegas is one of the most iconic and heavily visited themed hotels on the strip. The hotel is designed to look like the New York City skyline. In tribute to Coney Island and the famous Cyclone rollercoaster, a fully functioning rollercoaster goes around the outside of the hotel. A replica of the Statue of Liberty guards the hotel.

**Best Time to Visit:** The New York, New York Hotel is open and accessible all year round.

**Pass/Permit/Fees:** It is free to enter the hotel and the casino, but you must pay to ride the Big Apple Coaster. During the day, it is $19, and at night, it is $23. Additional rides cost $10.

**Closest City or Town:** Las Vegas

**How to Get There:** From I-515 N, take Exit 76A to get on I-15 S toward Los Angeles. Use the left lanes to stay on I-15 for 4.5 miles. Take Exit 37 for W. Tropicana Avenue. Make a U-turn at Dean Martin Drive, then turn left. The hotel is on the right at 3790 S. Las Vegas Boulevard.

**GPS Coordinates:** 36.1021° N, -115.1744° W

**Did You Know?** The United States Postal Service released a stamp of the Lady Liberty replica from the New York, New York Hotel.

## Paris Hotel and the Eiffel Tower

The Paris Hotel is home to French restaurants and a creperie, and the décor is all traditional French facades and styles. The Eiffel Tower replica located outside the hotel is half the size of the one in France and clearly visible from the Strip. The two back legs of the Eiffel Tower go down into the hotel and casino. There is a restaurant inside of the tower, and the rest of the décor in the hotel resembles the Arc de Triomphe, the Montgolfier balloon, and the Fontaine des Mers.

**Best Time to Visit:** The Paris Hotel is open and accessible all year round.

**Pass/Permit/Fees:** It is free to enter the Paris Hotel and Casino.

**Closest City or Town:** Las Vegas

**How to Get There:** The Paris Hotel is located on the Strip at 3655 S. Las Vegas Boulevard.

**GPS Coordinates:** 36.1125° N, -115.1707° W

**Did You Know?** The Eiffel Tower replica was originally supposed to be to scale. The city would not allow it to be so big because it would have interfered with air traffic flying into and out of McCarran International Airport.

# Red Rock Canyon

Red Rock Canyon National Conservation Area is 195,819 acres of wilderness. The area gets over two million visitors a year. Located just outside of Las Vegas, the park gets its name from the color of the Aztec sandstone. Millions of years ago, the area was once a deep sea, and the canyon was on the bottom of the ocean.

Aztec sandstone is red due to the presence of iron oxide and hematite. Over time, these elements rusted, which gives Red Rock Canyon its signature color. You can hike, camp, and explore Red Rock Canyon in any of the park's 26 areas.

**Best Time to Visit:** Red Rock Canyon is accessible all year round.

**Pass/Permit/Fees:** It costs $15 to enter Red Rock Canyon.

**Closest City or Town:** Las Vegas

**How to Get There:** From Las Vegas, get on I-515 N from N. 4th Street. Continue on US-95 N. Take NV-613 to NV-159 W. Take Exit 26 from County Road 215 S. Follow for 14.2 miles, then turn right onto NV-159 W. Follow for 1.5 miles to Red Rock Canyon National Conservation Area.

**GPS Coordinates:** 36.1944° N, -115.4383° W

**Did You Know?** Paleontologists have found dinosaur footprints in Red Rock! Other fossils, such as early mammals and spiders, have also been uncovered. It is still an active site for discovery and study.

# Sloan Canyon National Conservation Area

Sloan Canyon National Conservation Area is located in the southeastern part of Nevada, just outside of Las Vegas and Henderson. The area is 48,438 acres of wilderness. It is home to black volcanic mountains that can be seen from the neighboring cities. The canyon is also home to the Mohave green rattlesnake. Be alert because the snakes may be venomous. The area offers camping, hiking, and backpacking. It is a desert climate, so bring plenty of water for your stay.

**Best Time to Visit:** Sloan Canyon is accessible all year round, but it's best during the week when there are fewer people.

**Pass/Permit/Fees:** It is free to enter Sloan Canyon.

**Closest City or Town:** Las Vegas

**How to Get There:** From Las Vegas, get on I-515 S. Continue on I-515 S to Henderson. Take Exit 20 and continue for 15.2 miles, then follow to E. Horizon Ridge Parkway and E. Mission Drive to reach Sloan Canyon National Conservation Area.

**GPS Coordinates:** 35.9106° N, -115.0664° W

**Did You Know?** Sloan Canyon is home to the Petroglyph Trail. The area has 1,700 different petroglyph designs that depict the life of natives who once lived in the area. You will be able to see over 300 art panels on your hike.

# Spring Mountains

Offering spectacular views and shady valleys, The Spring Mountains were a massive draw for settlers and prospectors. Over the years, the range has developed into a recreational area. This mountain location has been home to many people, including famous German movie star Vera Krupp and American movie mogul Howard Hughes. The mountains offer hiking, camping, climbing, and backpacking, as well as an array of wildlife and wildflowers. Large animals like mule deer, bighorn sheep, bobcats, and mountain lions prowl the area. However, these big cats are rarely seen.

**Best Time to Visit:** Spring Mountain is accessible all year round.

**Pass/Permit/Fees:** It costs $10 to enter the Spring Mountains Recreation Area. It costs $15 for non-Nevada vehicles.

**Closest City or Town:** Las Vegas

**How to Get There:** From Las Vegas, follow I-15 S and NV-160 W to Trout Canyon Road in Nye County. Follow for 53.3 miles, then turn right onto Trout Canyon Road. Follow for 11.7 miles until you reach the Spring Mountains.

**GPS Coordinates:** 36.2100° N, -115.7056° W

**Did You Know?** The mountains are made out of limestone, which was deposited when the area was a deep sea about 400 million years ago.

# Stratosphere Tower

The Strat Hotel, Casino, and SkyPod is one of the most easily recognized hotels in Las Vegas. The hotel contains the 1,149-foot-tall Stratosphere Tower. You will get 360° panoramic views of Las Vegas and the surrounding mountains when you reach the top. There is also a revolving restaurant and lounges. The most stunning part of the tower is the collection of thrill rides at the top. The Big Shot is a ride that shoots you 160 feet up in the air to the top of the sky pod to a total height of 1,081 feet from the ground. Insanity dangles visitors over the edge of the tower 900 feet in the air. The most popular ride is the X-Scream, a rollercoaster that goes around the top of the tower and briefly dangles thrill-seekers over the edge 866 feet above the ground.

**Best Time to Visit:** The Stratosphere Tower is open all year round.

**Pass/Permit/Fees:** It costs $29 to access the observation decks.

**Closest City or Town:** Las Vegas

**How to Get There:** Take Las Vegas Boulevard S until you see the colossal observation tower at the end of the Strip.

**GPS Coordinates:** 36.1473° N, -115.1553° W

**Did You Know?** The Stratosphere Tower was almost the tallest observation tower in the world. It is the tallest observation tower in the United States and second in the western hemisphere next to the CN Tower in Toronto.

# Thai Buddhist Temple of Las Vegas

The Thai Buddhist Temple of Las Vegas is a popular temple for Buddhist practitioners. Although it may look unassuming from the outside, the inside of the temple is adorned with golden statues set amongst beds of flowers, adding another colorful touch to this sanctuary of peace. The exterior of the temple has several areas where you can meditate. Each area is set up like an altar space to provide a quiet environment to sit and reflect. Buddhist monks are always at the temple and will help you on your journey of quiet reflection.

**Best Time to Visit:** The Thai Buddhist Temple is available all year round.

**Pass/Permit/Fees:** It is free to enter the temple.

**Closest City or Town:** Las Vegas

**How to Get There:** From the strip, take I-15 N to Exit 42A/Martin Luther King Boulevard. Turn left onto W. Cheyenne Avenue, then right onto Simmons Street. Turn left onto W. Gowan Road, where you will see the temple.

**GPS Coordinates:** 36.2242° N, -115.1803° W

**Did You Know?** The monks have been known to share advice, food, and drink with those who grace their temple.

# The Mob Museum

Located in downtown Las Vegas, the Mob Museum's mission is to bring to light the many ways that organized crime has affected American society. The museum has hundreds of artifacts and exhibits that tell how the government and local police authorities fought with organized crime leaders across the land. The museum is set up for you to start at the museum's top floor and work your way down. The floors are broken up into the birth of the mob, the rise of the mob, and the mob on the run. There are interactive exhibits like a police line-up, the Valentine's Day Massacre wall, courtrooms, and a gun-training simulator.

**Best Time to Visit:** The Mob Museum is open year-round.

**Pass/Permit/Fees:** General admission is $29.95. There are other passes for admission and experiences that range from $41.95 to $48.95.

**Closest City or Town:** Las Vegas

**How to Get There:** You can take I-515 S to Stewart Avenue, where you will find the museum. From the Strip, take S. Las Vegas Boulevard N, then turn left onto Stewart Avenue.

**GPS Coordinates:** 36.1728° N, -115.1412° W

**Did You Know?** The basement of the Mob Museum is called the Underground. It includes a distillery and speakeasy dedicated to Prohibition-era bars.

## The Planetarium

Located on the campus of the College of Southern Nevada, the planetarium offers private and public viewings. The planetarium provides several shows that tell the story of the galaxy from creation to the present day. The performances are an immersive experience, launching visitors into outer space.

The shows at the planetarium change throughout the year, so you can visit several times to learn more about the Earth, the planets of the solar system, and our effects on both. All shows are projected on the planetarium's 30-foot dome from an Evans & Sutherland Digistar 5 projection system.

**Best Time to Visit:** The planetarium is available all year round. The shows are on Fridays and Saturdays.

**Pass/Permit/Fees:** General admission costs $6. Check the website for show ticket prices as these vary.

**Closest City or Town:** Las Vegas

**How to Get There:** From Las Vegas, take I-15 N to Exit 46 for Cheyenne Avenue. Turn left onto Campus Drive, and the planetarium will be on your right.

**GPS Coordinates:** 36.1314° N, -115.6150° W

**Did You Know?** The planetarium at the College of Southern Nevada is the only public planetarium in the southern part of the state.

# Valley of Fire State Park

The Valley of Fire State Park was formed millions of years ago when the area was still a sea. There are several hiking trails throughout the park. People have their weddings here, and filmmakers use the fire-red landscape for scenes that are set on Mars.

With so many points of interest, the Valley of Fire has something for everyone. With 13 nature spots to stop and see, you will find a lot of what makes Nevada so beautiful. At night, it gets so dark that you can see some of the most beautiful stargazing in America. Tours are available through the park for up to 8 people. They range in price from $300–$500.

**Best Time to Visit:** Valley of Fire State Park is open all year round.

**Pass/Permit/Fees:** It costs $10 to enter Valley of Fire State Park and $20 to camp.

**Closest City or Town:** Las Vegas

**How to Get There:** From Las Vegas, get on I-515 N/US-95 N from N. 4th Street. Follow I-15 N to your destination. Take Exit 75 from I-15 N. Continue for 33.3 miles, and merge onto Valley of Fire Highway. Drive for 11.8 miles until you arrive at Valley of Fire State Park.

**GPS Coordinates:** 36.5073° N, -114.5352° W

**Did You Know?** In the 1930s, cabins were constructed out of canyon rock for travelers to stay.

# Venetian Hotel and Gondola Rides

The Venetian's theme is all in its name: Venice. The hotel is designed to look like you are walking through the canals, shopping, and taking in Italian culture. The ceiling is painted to look like a beautiful blue sky, and along with shops and restaurants that lean towards Italian fare, you can also find some of the best gelato in Las Vegas. The most compelling part of the hotel is that a real canal runs through, offering gondola rides. The gondolier wears a traditional Venetian costume and may even sing Italian opera on your tour.

**Best Time to Visit:** The hotel and the gondola ride are open all year round.

**Pass/Permit/Fees:** The hotel lobby, casino, and shops are free. However, a gondola ride costs $29 per person from Monday through Thursday and $36 per person from Friday through Sunday.

**Closest City or Town:** Las Vegas

**How to Get There:** The hotel's address is 3355 S. Las Vegas Boulevard, located across the street from the Mirage Hotel.

**GPS Coordinates:** 36.1212° N, -115.1697° W

**Did You Know?** Artists flew in from around the world to make the hotel as authentic to Venice as possible. A green stone from the Italian Alps called Verde St. Denis is found throughout the hotel as a nod towards its Italian heritage.

# Cathedral Gorge

Formed from volcanic explosions millions of years ago, Cathedral Gorge State Park is in the southeastern part of Nevada. The hard rock was once a layer of thick ash hundreds of feet wide left behind by eruptions. Cathedral Gorge gets its name because the formations look like the spires of cathedrals. The park is a favorite spot for photography, hiking, and walking due to the picturesque geological structures. Overnight camping is allowed here.

**Best Time to Visit:** Cathedral Gorge is accessible and open all year round.

**Pass/Permit/Fees:** It costs $5 to enter Cathedral Gorge and $10 for non-Nevada vehicles to park.

**Closest City or Town:** Panaca

**How to Get There:** From Panaca, head north onto S. 5th Street toward NV-319 E. Turn left at the first cross street onto NV-319 W, then make a right onto US-93 N. Turn left onto Cathedral Gorge State Park Road.

**GPS Coordinates:** 37.8241° N, -114.4155° W

**Did You Know?** Some of the trails go through caves and gorges throughout the park, allowing you to get up close and personal with the rock formations.

# Humboldt-Toiyabe National Forest

Humboldt-Toiyabe National Forest is the largest national forest in the lower 48 states. It contains 6.3 million acres of land that stretch from California through Nevada to the borders of Idaho and Utah. Because of its vastness, you can do practically any outdoor activity in Humboldt-Toiyabe State Forest. It is most known for its various wilderness areas, the most popular being Hoover Wilderness. There are also canyons throughout the forest and mountains for hiking, climbing, and backpacking. The park contains 80,000 to 100,000 archaeological sites.

**Best Time to Visit:** Humboldt-Toiyabe National Forest is accessible all year round.

**Pass/Permit/Fees:** It costs $9 to get permits to Humboldt-Toiyabe National Forest.

**Closest City or Town:** Sparks

**How to Get There:** From Sparks, take I-80 W to Exit 15. Merge onto I-580 S. Keep left to stay on I-580 S until you can take a left onto US-395 S. Take a right onto Jacks Valley Road. In 2.4 miles, the forest will be on the right at 3450 Jacks Valley Drive.

**GPS Coordinates:** 39.1060° N, -119.8149° W

**Did You Know?** The forest is also a habitat for several species. Various ghost towns and ghost mines are spread throughout the region.

# Seven Troughs Distilling Company

Seven Troughs Distilling Company is steeped in the local mining traditions from over 100 years ago. Its namesake is derived from a small mining town, which was founded around 1905. Between 1908 and 1921, the town produced over $2 million in gold. It was fully abandoned during the Great Depression. The distillery uses a mid-19th century fermentation process for making moonshine in honor of the old mining town. The same fermentation process is used when the distillery makes vodka, gin, rum, and bourbon.

**Best Time to Visit:** Seven Troughs Distillery is available all year round during normal business hours.

**Pass/Permit/Fees:** Normally, the distillery has no cover charge, but it does cost to attend special events.

**Closest City or Town:** Sparks

**How to Get There:** In Sparks, head west on Victorian Avenue. Turn left at the first cross street onto Pyramid Way. Turn left onto Nugget Avenue, then take a right onto S. McCarran Blvd. Turn left onto E. Glendale Avenue and right onto Watson Way. The distillery is on the right at 1155 Watson Way.

**GPS Coordinates:** 39.5249° N, -119.7342° W

**Did You Know?** The Seven Troughs Distillery has a speakeasy. To enter the speakeasy, you must follow a detailed map of several twists and turns within the neighborhood until you come to a marked door that takes you down another corridor into the speakeasy.

# Sparks Heritage Museum

The Sparks Heritage Museum details the history of Sparks and all of the changes in northern Nevada. Northern Nevada is an area with a colorful history, starting with the Gold Rush and mining days, followed by ranching and the railroad. The museum also has modern exhibits that relate to the people of the area. Some of the outdoor exhibits include preserved train cars from the early 20th century; the Glendale Schoolhouse, which was created in 1864 and was the school that Nevada senator Pat McCarran attended; and two exhibits honoring the Chinese immigrants who worked on the railroad.

**Best Time to Visit:** The museum is available all year round, Tuesday through Saturday.

**Pass/Permit/Fees:** Visitors 12 and older cost $8; visitors ages 2–11 cost $5. There is a membership program, and donations are accepted.

**Closest City or Town:** Sparks

**How to Get There:** The museum is located at 814 Victorian Avenue.

**GPS Coordinates:** 39.5351° N, -119.7533° W

**Did You Know?** Sparks Museum is home to Last Chance Joe, a 36-foot-tall statue that once stood in front of the Nugget Casino. In recent years, the museum has had problems keeping Joe and is currently seeking ways to preserve the 60-year-old statue.

# Rail City Casino

Rail City Casino opened in the late 1970s as the Plantation Casino. It is a popular place for adults to hang out, eat, and gamble. The casino offers Rail City Ale and a buffet. Rail City has seven table games and almost 900 slot machines. There is also a keno parlor and off-track betting. Although this is not a place to bring kids, it's ideal if you are traveling with adults. The casino almost didn't get its license to open because one owner was a known friend of criminals. It went through a change of ownership in the 1990s and was renamed Rail City.

**Best Time to Visit:** Rail City Casino is open year round.

**Pass/Permit/Fees:** There is no cover charge, only fees for gambling and food.

**Closest City or Town:** Sparks

**How to Get There:** In Sparks, head west on Victorian Avenue. Turn left onto 21st St. Take a right in 187 feet. Take another right, and the casino will be on the right at 2121 Victorian Ave.

**GPS Coordinates:** 39.5349° N, -119.7722° W

**Did You Know?** The gaming commission almost shut down Rail City Casino when it was found that the owners were using counterfeit coins in the slot machines.

## Revision Brewing Company

Revision Brewing Company was founded in 2015 and was initially supposed to open in West Sacramento, California. After the West Sacramento location fell through, Revision opened in 2016 in Sparks. By early March 2017, the beer was on its way to bars and markets. The brewery opened to guests, and by late spring, it was a popular spot for locals and visitors to gather. By 2019, the beer made it overseas. Since it started selling beer in 2017, Revision has received several beer awards in both the United States and abroad.

**Best Time to Visit:** Revision Brewing Company is open and accessible all year round.

**Pass/Permit/Fees:** There is no cover charge to enter Revision Brewery.

**Closest City or Town:** Sparks

**How to Get There:** In Sparks, head west on Victorian Avenue toward Pyramid Way. Turn left at the first cross street onto Pyramid Way. Merge onto I-80 W toward Reno. Take Exit 17 for Rock Boulevard. Turn left onto S. Rock Boulevard. The brewery is on the left at 380 S. Rock Boulevard.

**GPS Coordinates:** 39.5312° N, -119.7659° W.

**Did You Know?** Revision is marketed as being hop forward, so there is some bitterness to the beers. If you like hoppy beers, Revision is a great place to try some.

# Lunar Crater National Natural Landmark

Lunar Crater is one of six natural landmarks in the state of Nevada. The crater was formed by ground-level volcanic explosions, which is why the cavity is so vast and shallow. The proper term for a crater of this kind is *maar*. Located in the Pancake Range, the maar was deemed a natural landmark in 1973. The maar is located in the desert and is usually not too crowded if you want to visit. You can camp or walk around the rim, and some even take the relatively easy hike down into the crater itself. It is not recommended to bring your dogs for safety purposes.

**Best Time to Visit:** Accessible all year round, Lunar Crater is best from spring through the fall.

**Pass/Permit/Fees:** There are no fees to access Lunar Crater.

**Closest City or Town:** Tonopah

**How to Get There:** Lunar Crater is off the beaten path, and the road to get there is long. Many streets do not have signs as they are small roads that go through the desert. The best way to get there is from the north via Highway 6 to the Lunar Crater Backcountry Byway. It is a little trickier from the south as you take the "Extraterrestrial Highway" through barren country. Bring a map and study the route in advance.

**GPS Coordinates:** 38.3840° N, -116.0697° W

**Did You Know?** Lunar Crater was the training site of the Apollo 16 and Apollo 17 moon missions.

## Animal Ark

Located 30 miles north of Reno, you will find Animal Ark, a sanctuary for injured, aged, and abandoned wildlife that cannot reintegrate into the wild. The mission of Animal Ark is to provide education on wildlife to help save the species that seek refuge within its walls. Animal Ark has a wide variety of wildlife, including foxes, hawks, turtles, cheetahs, tigers, bears, and porcupines. The animals are primarily North American predators and small wildlife. The sanctuary studies these animals while caring for them to learn more about how they live and protect various species from extinction.

**Best Time to Visit:** Animal Ark is open year round. It is closed on Mondays.

**Pass/Permit/Fees:** Tickets for Animal Ark are $14 for adults, $12 for seniors, and $9 for children ages 3–12.

**Closest City or Town:** Reno

**How to Get There:** From Reno, take I-80 E to Exit 15 to merge onto US-395 N. Take Exit 78, and turn right onto Red Rock Road. Turn right on Deerlodge Road, where you will find the sanctuary.

**GPS Coordinates:** 39.7839° N, -119.8690° W

**Did You Know?** The best time to visit the sanctuary is first thing in the morning during feeding time because that's when the nocturnal animals are still awake, and you will be able to see all the animals in the sanctuary.

# Bowers Mansion Regional Park

Bowers Mansion Regional Park is located just south of Reno on the edge of the Sierra Mountains. The park houses Bower Mansion, which was built in 1864. The home is named after its builders and inhabitants, L.S. Bowers and his psychic wife Eilley. They made their fortune mining for silver and became two of Nevada's first millionaires. The rest of the park is popular for picnics and wildlife viewing. There is a plethora of trees in the park and several pavilions for picnics and gatherings. There is also a large swimming pool. Pets are not allowed in the park.

**Best Time to Visit:** Bowers Mansion Regional Park is available all year round, but the best time to visit is in the summer when the pool is open.

**Pass/Permit/Fees:** It is free to enter the park, but you must pay to use the pool. To take a tour of the mansion, adults cost $8 and children cost $5.

**Closest City or Town:** Reno

**How to Get There:** From Reno, take I-580 S. Use Exit 16 to get onto Old US-395. From the highway, turn onto County Road 330, and continue until you reach the parking lot at 4005 Bowers Mansion Road.

**GPS Coordinates:** 39.2851° N, -119.8418° W

**Did You Know?** The park offers an outdoor escape room. You can follow clues throughout the park to solve the riddles and complete your quest.

# National Automobile Museum

Located in Reno, the National Automobile Museum displays classic cars in unique and creative ways. In addition to showcasing car makes and models throughout history, the museum also acts as a special events venue. The museum has several rooms where cityscapes surround the featured car with sounds and artifacts so that onlookers can see what life may have looked like when that particular car was on the road. On Science Saturday, visitors can learn about the solar system. There are virtual reality headsets that take you on a journey through space.

**Best Time to Visit:** The museum is open all year round.

**Pass/Permit/Fees:** It costs $12 to enter the museum. The cost for senior citizens is $10. Children ages 6–18 cost $6, and children under 6 are free.

**Closest City or Town:** Reno

**How to Get There:** In Reno, head south on Old US-395 N. Turn left onto E. Commercial Row, then take a right onto Lake Street. Turn left onto Tahoe-Pyramid Bikeway. Turn right onto Museum Drive. Take another right, and the museum will be on the right at 10 South Lake Street.

**GPS Coordinates:** 39.5259° N, -119.8088° W

**Did You Know?** The National Automobile Museum is also an event space designed for corporate events, speed networking, proms, graduations, and even weddings.

## National Bowling Stadium

The National Bowling Stadium opened in 1995, and many refer to it as the Taj Mahal of Tenpins. It cost $47.5 million to build and was part of the renovation of downtown Reno. There is an 80-foot aluminum dome on the front that represents a bowling ball. The stadium is used for national and international bowling tournaments. At the time of its construction, it had one of the largest backlight video screens. It is also an extension of the International Bowling Museum. Visitors can see portraits of bowlers in the hall of fame, and there are several bowling artifacts on display. The stadium is the location for almost all bowling scenes filmed in Hollywood movies.

**Best Time to Visit:** The National Bowling Stadium is open all year round, 24 hours per day.

**Pass/Permit/Fees:** It is free to enter the museum. The stadium is open to the public when there are events. Event tickets vary in price, so it is best to check the website prior to visiting.

**Closest City or Town:** Reno

**How to Get There:** Head north on Old US-395 N. Turn right onto E. 4th Street, then turn right again onto N. Center Street. The stadium is on the left at 300 N. Center Street.

**GPS Coordinates:** 39.5296° N, -119.8123° W

**Did You Know?** The original stadium had 80 bowling lanes, but an architectural error left out an entrance aisle for competitors, so two lanes were removed, leaving 78 lanes.

## Nevada Historical Society Museum

The Nevada Historical Society Museum is the home of artifacts and history for the state of Nevada. The American Gaming Archives are located in the museum as well as other exhibitions and artifacts revolving around Native Americans in Nevada. The artifacts on display tell the story of how Native Americans survived in the Great Basin. Other items at the museum chronicle the history of gold and silver mining, the building of the American railroad, and the birth of the modern era.

**Best Time to Visit:** The museum is available all year round, Wednesday through Friday. Appointments are required to visit on Thursdays and Fridays. The museum is closed on state and federal holidays.

**Pass/Permit/Fees:** Members and children under 18 years of age are free. Non-member adults cost $5.

**Closest City or Town:** Reno

**How to Get There:** When in Reno, you can find the museum on N. Virginia Street next to the Fleischmann Planetarium.

**GPS Coordinates:** 39.5486° N, -119.8204° W

**Did You Know?** The Nevada Historical Society Museum is the oldest museum in Nevada.

# Nevada Museum of Art

The Nevada Museum of Art houses 19th-century, 20th-century, and modern art. The museum's exhibitions feature artwork by some of the most prominent artists of today. Much of the art depicts the human experience interacting with nature. The museum's permanent collections offer over 2,000 pieces of art that represent virtual, constructed, or natural environments from throughout the world. They speak of the world's landscape and man's role in its development or destruction. The museum offers several art classes instituted by the Center for Art and Environment. All the art and topics discussed aim to bring together man and nature.

**Best Time to Visit:** The Nevada Museum of Art is open all year round. It is closed on Mondays and major holidays.

**Pass/Permit/Fees:** It costs $10 to enter the museum. Students and seniors cost $8, and it costs $1 for children 6–12 years old. Children under 6 get in free.

**Closest City or Town:** Reno

**How to Get There:** Head south on Old US-395 S. Turn right onto W. 3rd Street, then left on N. Sierra Street. Turn right onto W. Liberty Street. Make a left, and the museum will be on the right at 160 West Liberty Street.

**GPS Coordinates:** 39.5208° N, -119.8134° W

**Did You Know?** The museum gives out Scholastic Art Awards to children in northern Nevada while also providing art classes and skill-building for teachers.

# Oxbow Nature Study Area

Located just outside Reno, Oxbow Nature Study Area is recognized as an urban nature center. The Nevada Department of Wildlife hosts Wildlife and Aquatic Education programs that have become a public model for wilderness education. These programs play an important role in Nevada's nature conservation efforts.

Oxbow is one of the best areas for families to walk and see nature. There is a trail in Oxbow that is about one mile long and loops around the pond. While on that path, you can see all the animals, plants, and trees.

**Best Time to Visit:** Oxbow Nature Study Area is open all year round, every day.

**Pass/Permit/Fees:** It is free to enter Oxbow Nature Study Area.

**Closest City or Town:** Reno

**How to Get There:** From Reno, head north on Old US-395 N toward E. 4th Street. Turn left at the first cross street onto W. 4th Street. Turn left onto Ralston Street, then right onto W. 2nd Street. Continue onto Dickerson Road. Oxbow Nature Study Area will be on the left.

**GPS Coordinates:** 39.5188° N, -119.8466° W

**Did You Know?** The study area is home to rainbow trout, mule deer, black-crowned night herons, and red-shouldered hawks.

# Pioneer Center for the Performing Arts

A historical landmark, the Pioneer Center for the Performing Arts opened in the late 1960s during a cultural renaissance in Reno. At the time, Reno's tourist industry was growing, and the city invested in cultural and entertainment venues. Originally named the Pioneer Theater – Auditorium, the Pioneer Center was opened as a home for dance, acting, music, comedy, and concerts. Broadway shows tour through the center, as do many famous and successful artists.

**Best Time to Visit:** The Pioneer Center is open year round.

**Pass/Permit/Fees:** Tickets to the center vary based on the performance. Check the website for prices.

**Closest City or Town:** Reno

**How to Get There:** In Reno, head south on US-395 N toward Plaza Street for 0.4 miles. Turn left onto State Street, and the center will be on the left at 100 S. Virginia Street.

**GPS Coordinates:** 39.5243° N, -119.8114° W

**Did You Know?** The center is called the Pioneer Center after a statue of a pioneer family heading west in front of the building. The building is also called the "Golden Turtle" because of the geometric dome that makes it look like a turtle's shell.

# Pyramid Lake

Pyramid Lake is a large desert lake located just outside of Reno in the northwestern part of Nevada. The lake has a rich history dating back to prehistoric times. It was the home of Native American tribes who used the lake for sustenance and a place to set up villages. The lake offers fishing, swimming, boating, and camping.

The Native American tribe, the Paiute, has a deep history on the lake, and the tribe continues to practice traditions and celebrations all year round. There is a museum near the water where you can learn the history of the Native American tribe, the lake, and its geological formation. Pyramid Lake received its name from a tufa formation that looks like a pyramid in the lake's center. A tufa consists of limestone that forms in ambient waters.

**Best Time to Visit:** Pyramid Lake is accessible all year round.

**Pass/Permit/Fees:** It is $22 for day use, and there are permits and fees required for boating, fishing, and camping.

**Closest City or Town:** Reno

**How to Get There:** From Reno, follow NV-445 N for 40.6 miles until you reach Windless Beach on Pyramid Lake.

**GPS Coordinates:** 49.99882° N, -119.62529° W

**Did You Know?** Pyramid Lake is the last remnant of the prehistoric Lake Lahontan.

# Reno Arch

The Reno Arch is a landmark that is known all across the United States. The arch goes over Virginia Street at the crossing of Commercial Row in downtown Reno. The idea for the arch was sparked in the late 1920s when the Victory and Lincoln highways were completed. The arch was created in commemoration of that remarkable feat. When the highways were completed (today's highways 50 and 80), the city hosted an exposition, and the arch was placed for the gathering. A week after the celebration, the city decided to keep the arch permanently. There was a slogan contest to choose the city's slogan. G.A. Burns won the contest and received $100 for "Reno: The Biggest Little City in the World!" The slogan appeared in 1929 and remains there today.

**Best Time to Visit:** The Reno Arch is on full display 24 hours a day, seven days a week.

**Pass/Permit/Fees:** It is free to drive or walk underneath the arch.

**Closest City or Town:** Reno,

**How to Get There:** In Reno, you can access the arch from Old US-395 N at the intersection of Virginia Street and Commerce Row at 345 N. Virginia Street.

**GPS Coordinates:** 39.5282° N, -119.8137° W

**Did You Know?** The sign for Reno Arch has changed three times in the past 100 years,

# Virginia and Truckee Railway

The Virginia and Truckee Railway was built in the 19th century for the sole purpose of hauling commercial loads across Nevada. The original path the railway took was from Reno to the state capital of Carson City. At Carson City, the railway then split, and one branch went to Minden while the other went to Virginia City. Most of the haul was to bring supplies to the silver mines in the state. In the 1950s, there was no longer any use for the railroad, so it was torn up and sold. By the 1970s, interest reemerged, and the railway was rebuilt for historical purposes.

**Best Time to Visit:** The railway is available all year round.

**Pass/Permit/Fees:** Tickets to ride the Virginia and Truckee Railway cost $14 per person. Children ages 5–12 cost $7, and children under 5 ride for free.

**Closest City or Town:** Reno

**How to Get There:** From Reno, take I-80 to I-580 S. Take Exit 25B onto State Highway 341 E, which will take you into Virginia City via Taylor Street. Take Taylor Street to F Street, where you will find the entrance to the railroad.

**GPS Coordinates:** 39.2031° N, -119.6794° W

**Did You Know?** The locomotive you will ride on is the V&T Railway featured in the Hollywood movie *Water for Elephants.*

# Wilson Canyon Park

Wilson Canyon is a vast gorge that formed as a result of several prehistoric volcanic explosions. The canyon is a popular site for camping, hiking, and climbing. The most common sports in the canyon are off-roading and dirt biking, as the desert terrain and sand make for ideal conditions. It is a popular getaway for many locals. The Walker River runs through the canyon and is a known fishing spot. The river is fed by snowmelt from the Sierra Nevada range and flows about 62 miles into the Walker Lake watershed. This watershed is 3,082 square miles and occupies the most significant part of Walker Lake.

**Best Time to Visit:** The best time to plan your visit at Wilson Canyon is November through June, when the weather is not too hot.

**Pass/Permit/Fees:** It is free to enter Wilson Canyon.

**Closest City or Town:** Yerington

**How to Get There:** From Yerington, head west on Pacific Street toward S. Main Street. Turn left at the first cross street onto S. Main Street. Turn right after Wells Fargo Bank. In 1 mile, turn left onto NV-339 S. In 10.7 miles, take a sharp left onto NV-208 E. Turn right onto Wilson Canyon Drive.

**GPS Coordinates:** 38.8102° N, -119.2273° W

**Did You Know?** Wilson Canyon is comprised primarily of volcanic cliffs that were formed millions of years ago.

## *Proper Planning*

With this guide, you are well on your way to properly planning a marvelous adventure. When you plan your travels, you should become familiar with the area, save any maps to your phone for access without internet, and bring plenty of water—especially during summer months. Depending on the adventure you choose, you will also want to bring snacks and even a lunch. For younger children, you should do your research and find destinations that best suits the needs of your family. Additionally, you should also plan when to get gas, scout local lodgings, and figure out where to get food after you're finished. We've done our best to group these destinations based on nearby towns and cities to help make planning easier.

*Dangerous Wildlife*

There are several dangerous animals and insects you may encounter while hiking. With a good dose of caution and awareness, you can explore safely. Here is what you can do to keep yourself and your loved ones safe from dangerous flora and fauna while exploring:

- Keep to the established trails.
- Do not look under rocks, leaves, or sticks.
- Keep hands and feet out of small crawl spaces, bushes, covered areas, or crevices.
- Wear long sleeves and pants to keep arms and legs protected.
- Keep your distance should you encounter any dangerous wildlife or plants.

*Limited Cell Service*

Do not rely on cell service for navigation or emergencies. Always have a map with you, and let someone know where you are and for how long you intend to be gone, just in case.

*First Aid Information*

Always travel with a first aid kit with you in case of emergencies. Here are items that you should be certain to include in your primary first aid kit:

- Nitrile gloves
- Blister care products
- Waterproof bandages in multiple sizes
- Ace wrap and athletic tape
- Alcohol wipes and antibiotic ointment
- Irrigation syringe
- Tweezers, nail clippers, trauma shears, safety pins
- Small Ziplock bags for holding contaminated trash

It's a good practice to also keep a secondary first aid kit, especially when hiking, for more serious injuries or medical emergencies. Items in this should include:

- Blood clotting sponges
- Sterile gauze pads
- Trauma pads
- Moist burn pads
- Triangular bandages/sling
- Butterfly strips
- Tincture of benzoin
- Medications (ibuprofen, acetaminophen, antihistamine, aspirin, etc.)
- Thermometer

- CPR mask
- Wilderness medicine handbook
- Antivenin

***There is so much more to explore***, but this is a great start.

For information on all national parks, visit: www.nps.gov.

This site will give you information on up-to-date entrance fees and how to purchase a park pass for unlimited access to national and state parks. These sites will also introduce you to all of the trails of each park.

Always check before you travel to destinations to make sure that there are no closures. Some hikes close when there is heavy rain or snow in the area, and other parks close parts of their land to allow wildlife to migrate. Attractions may change their hours or temporarily shut down for various reasons. Check the websites for the most up-to-date information.

Made in the USA
Thornton, CO
12/10/24 09:14:33

917b0cf4-d66f-4d11-92ac-89e2575b97e9R01